How my Husband

Keeps me H♥ppy

How my Husband
Keeps me H♥ppy

*A Guide To Building
A Marriage That Lasts
For Husbands (and Wives Too!)*

Karen Gordon & Evan Myshrall

BrightFlame
Books By Experts

Copyright © 2016 by Karen Gordon & Evan Myshrall. All rights reserved.

First Edition. Published in Canada by BrightFlame Books, Burlington, Ontario. www.BrightFlameBooks.com

No part of this book may be used or reproduced in any manner whatsoever without written permission except in the case of brief quotations embodied in critical reviews and articles in their entirety.

Limit of Liability/Disclaimer of Warranty: The information in this book is presented for entertainment purposes only. The publisher and authors make no representations or warranties with respect to the accuracy or completeness of the information contained in this work and specifically disclaim any implied warranties of merchantability or fitness for a particular purpose. No warranty may be created or extended by sales representatives or written sales materials. The advice and strategies contained herein may not be suitable for your situation. You should consult with a qualified professional adviser where appropriate. Neither the publisher nor the author shall be liable for any loss of income, profit or any other commercial damages, nor any emotional or psychological distress, including but not limited to special, incidental, consequential, or other damages.

Photography by: Stan Switalski (www.stanswitalski.com)

ISBN (Paperback): 978-1-988179-21-6
ISBN (Hardback): 978-1-988179-25-4
ISBN (Kindle): 978-1-988179-22-3

Dedication

To our grandparents, parents, aunts, uncles, brothers, sisters, cousins, many friends and all who have been relationship role models for us.

Acknowledgements

We want to acknowledge the many people who have been involved in our lives.

We have been blessed with many friends, who have supported us over the years, including the following people, who were a support network for Evan: Lianne McDonald, Jill McRae, Ann Stephens, and Chris and Cindy Charbonneau.

Our huge extended family, who we love and adore.

Our many role models, starting with Evan's father, Orlo Myshrall. He became Evan's stepfather when he was 7 years old but treated him like his own flesh and blood, and Evan has always considered him his true father.

Evan's younger brother John and his wife Nancy were there from the start to help Evan through his difficult separation and divorce. They opened up their home to Evan and his son.

Evan's mother, Shirley Myshrall, who was the first woman he loved when he came into this world and was his biggest supporter and go-to person when he needed a shoulder to cry on. Evan is the man he is today, because of her.

Evan's sister Kathy Brill, who we lovingly call "the brat." Their paths have often been parallel; they laugh at each other and adore each other's company and share a lot of similar stories. Like Evan, she went through a divorce but was able to find happiness with her next relationship: a man swept her off her feet, and has kept her there and cared for her.

To Aidan and Ryan, who filled the void in both our lives. If Aidan hadn't given Evan the green light to join eHarmony, we would never have met, and we would not have built the life we have.

To Gloria, Karen's mother, for encouraging her to join eHarmony. To both of Karen's parents, Gloria and Garth, who provided principles for supporting each other throughout a 47-year marriage that was cut short by cancer. To Nancy, for giving Karen's dad a second chance at love.

To Karen's sister Kelly and her husband Kent for their support and encouragement over the years.

Dr. Neil Clark Warren, the founder of eHarmony. His website has given us a second chance at life and happiness. We are truly grateful to have been given that gift.

Evan would like to thank *Pookie*: "Karen, you are my wife and best friend. If you hadn't answered my profile, I would not be here. I don't know where I would be without you."

Lastly, Karen would like to acknowledge Evan and all his efforts as the inspiration for this book: For, without you and the things that you do, the concept for this book would never have been created.

A Note on Language

We wanted this book to feel like a conversation with two ordinary people. We're not academics. We're not medical professionals or psychologists. We're not marriage counselors.

We are just two people who are very much in love and want to share our experience.

So, we'll occasionally say things like *kids* instead of *children* because that's how we speak.

One of the big challenges we faced was how to write a book from the point of view of two people.

In the end, most of the book is written as *us*, and we use a name if we have to refer to Evan or Karen individually (just like that!).

We wanted to keep things quite conversational, though, so in some places, one or other of us will be speaking to you directly to give their point of view on what we are describing.

> **KAREN:** When that happens, you'll see we introduce it with the name of the person speaking.

Table of Contents

Acknowledgements vii

A Note on Language xi

Introduction 1

Chapter 1
Keeping the Relationship Fresh 7

Chapter 2
Happy Wife, Happy Life 25

Chapter 3
Show Them You Care 39

Chapter 4
Listen (And Prove It) 49

Chapter 5
Let The World Know How Much You Love Her 61

Chapter 6
Evan's Story 67

Chapter 7
Make Each Other Laugh 81

Chapter 8
Commit To Making Her Feel Special 95

Chapter 9
Simple Things Score Big Points 103

Chapter 10
'Tis The Season To Be Stressful! 113

Chapter 11
So Many Ways To Communicate 123

Chapter 12
She's Number One 131

Chapter 13
Respect, Trust, and Loyalty 151

Chapter 14
Engage In Conversation 161

Chapter 15
The Little Things Go A Long Way 169

Chapter 16
QIQO 179

Chapter 17
Now We Are Cooking 195

Conclusion
Wrapping Up 201

Introduction

This is not a book of marriage guidance. For one thing, we would never hold ourselves up as a shining example of how everyone should live life. What we share in this book is simply what works for us, and it's made our marriage better than either of us could ever have imagined.

On our wedding day, our pastor told us that we had the ability to build our relationship into something that could be a model for others to look at and strive for. This book is, in many ways, our way of following through on that advice.

Evan's brother John added two further pieces of advice that we thought you'd enjoy because they give you some insight into the fun kind of relationship we have.

> Evan for Karen: Tell her you love her every day, shower her with gifts, fight for her, walk to the ends of the earth for her, tell her there is no other.

> Karen for Evan: Show up naked and bring beer!

Why We Wrote This Book

The main reason we wrote this book is that whenever we tell people about something that one of us has done for the other the response is almost always the same: "I wish my husband/wife/spouse/partner/etc. would do that for me!" And when we told people we were thinking of writing a book, they all said, "I want to read that book!" So now they can.

Will doing what we do and thinking how we think save a failed marriage? Maybe, but probably not, and we say that for a very good reason: we are both on our second marriage. While we may have grown as human beings over the years, we are still substantially the same people we were back then. Most of what we do now we also did in our respective first marriages, but for whatever reasons those marriages didn't work.

Will what we share help improve a marriage that is starting to shake? Probably. If you both want to make it better and make it work, but you're struggling for ideas to make that happen, then hopefully we can spark some thoughts that will help.

And will what we share help to make a good marriage even better? Absolutely. You may find that you already do a lot of the same things we do and think the way we think. Even so, as Evan says, he always reads manuals (even though he's a man) because there's always something new to learn or something you may need to be reminded about.

The days of stay-at-home wives as homemakers, while the husband goes out to work, are way behind us. Most couples these days are a partnership where both partners go out to work. They get very little downtime, especially if they have children.

Sometimes, one person in that partnership will be asking for help, but the other doesn't hear them or doesn't notice. So a lot of what we talk about in this book is simply learning to listen, but listen with all your senses.

Sometimes—and this is especially true for men—we need help, but we don't want to show emotion, and we don't want to seem weak, so we don't even ask for help.

> **EVAN:** I learned long ago to trust my emotions and not to be afraid to show them: your emotions will always lead you in the right direction, because *how we are feeling* is a much

> more reliable indicator of what we need than *what we are thinking.*

Before we met, Evan went through seven years of upheaval and turmoil. It was a dark time, and it left him exhausted.

> **EVAN:** My family, co-workers, and friends saw me come through that, and they saw my life transform when I met Karen. They saw me come full circle, from being a broken man whose entire world had been turned upside down by divorce to becoming healed and whole again.
>
> They always told me I should write a book and call it *A Man Against The Odds.* That would have been a very different book from the one you are holding now. I have done my best to avoid talking about the failure of my first marriage. Instead, Karen and I agreed to focus on what is working well in our relationship.
>
> I have a great circle of friends, and I want people to know that. In many ways, I've been given a second chance at life. To be given a second chance shows that there is a reason to have hope.

One of Evan's co-workers, Pam, is a single mother with a young son, just as Karen was. She hears him talk about our relationship, and she says that we give her hope.

So here are the key points that we want you to take away from this book, that we hope will help you to make your relationship stronger and better, and take it to the next level.

1. Listen. *Really* listen: hear what the other person is saying, take it on board, and think about what it means: for you and for them.

2. Act. Do something about what your partner is saying. You are not doing this out of idle interest: they are telling you what they need from you.

3. Invest. Marriage is a huge investment: of time, of energy and of emotion. Protect and keep contributing to your investment.

Chapter 1

Keeping the Relationship Fresh

One of the biggest challenges couples face is maintaining the excitement and the novelty they had when the relationship was new. After a while, it's easy to fall into 'life as usual' and stop making the kinds of efforts you made at the start. That's the top of a very slippery slope.

When a relationship is new, you talk, and you share, and you're constantly looking for new things to do together, which is easy because *everything* is new. Every day is full of surprises: you discover something you never knew about your partner, or you realize that you both have a shared love of a particular band or actor or writer, or you both had a similar experience in your past. And you want to get to know this person, so you share, and you communicate openly.

As time goes on, however, you get into a shared rhythm. There's less to discover together, fewer surprises, and the communication dries up.

If you feel like your marriage is headed that way, then you need to freshen things up and get that excitement back.

Emails in the dark

Karen's eyes fluttered open in the darkness. Groggily, she looked across at the glowing numbers on her alarm clock. 4:00. A few weeks before, she'd have rolled over and tried to get back to sleep, knowing she had a full day of work ahead of her.

But now, 4 in the morning was exciting. She didn't even need to set the alarm: her body knew when 4 a.m. came around and got her up.

She pushed the covers back and sat up on the edge of the bed, and walked out of the bedroom. Slowly, she made her way through the house, careful not to make any noise—she didn't want to wake Ryan up on a school night. Or should I say morning?

> *She opened the door to the spare room, where the computer was—an old clunky desktop that took so long to start up, most nights she would leave it running so it was ready at 4 a.m.*
>
> *The screen flickered back to life as Karen nudged the mouse to wake the computer out of standby. The mail icon on her desktop told her she had 20 unread emails, but she only really cared about one, and a thought crossed her mind: "I must be falling for this guy!"*

Our 4 a.m. email routine had been forced on us by two very different schedules.

> **EVAN:** Before we met, I had been working the weekend shift, which made seeing my son a challenge. I had access to Aidan every other weekend, and I was relying on family members and friends to pick him up from my ex-wife's house and look after him until I came home. After a few months of that, it became obvious it wasn't a sustainable situation. My boss knew I had fought tooth-and-nail to get those precious weekends with my son, but in the end,

> I had to threaten to resign in order to get my shift changed.
>
> So, when we met, I was working 3 p.m. 'til 11 p.m., Monday to Friday. That's not a very 'date friendly' arrangement, and to make things worse, most nights I wouldn't get home until 2 or 3 in the morning.
>
> And each night when I got home, the first thing I would do was email Karen.

To make things that little bit more complicated, we'd also decided not to introduce our sons to each other yet. We had to make sure we were compatible first. Neither of us wanted to put them through the wringer of "here's this new person in our lives," and then explaining a few weeks later why that new person wasn't there anymore. So we were seeing each other twice a month—basically on the weekends when Evan didn't have Aidan.

> **KAREN:** It was early November when we finally introduced them. We could tell by that point that we were compatible and I said, "we've got to let the kids meet each other." It was the only way we were going to be able to see each other more than twice a month!

And so, early in November, we all went to Springridge Farm and let the kids play in the hay and get to know each other. It was the first time Aidan and Ryan met each other, and also the first time Karen met Aidan.

Of course, even though this happened in the early days of our relationship, it could easily have happened later. Many couples find themselves separated by circumstances. Perhaps one of them gets a job that involves travel, or a family member falls ill and one of the spouses has to go and look after them while their partner stays home to hold the fort, or—as with Evan's job—they may get put onto a shift pattern that isn't family-friendly.

Keeping a relationship going in those circumstances takes patience and dedication. Even established couples would have struggled, and it would have been so easy for us to just say, "this is too hard," and give up. But something made us both want to keep going, to make it work. We both looked forward to our weekends together. We would go out for dinner, or go bowling, or whatever it might be. The key was to have something planned that we could look forward to— and that's something that we still do, as we'll explain elsewhere in the book.

It was our crazy lifestyle—only meeting every other weekend—that initially forced us to look for new ways to communicate. Email was only the first, but Evan quickly got more creative. So the nightly emails weren't just a rundown of the day's events. There'd be a quiz or a survey. Or he would create an ecard using a picture he'd found online.

> **KAREN:** Back then, we had both recently created accounts on Facebook. Quizzes were all the rage, and we had a blast completing and sharing the ones we found: "Look what I found! Try this one, it's really cool."

The quizzes were simple, fun ones, just to see how the other person thinks: "Pick a color. What's your favorite tree? Cat or dog? Ice or no ice?" and then we'd compare answers.

For the most part, our answers were the same or very close. That's hardly surprising, since we had both filled out the eHarmony profile, and we knew we were compatible. But it can be fun to put a score on your compatibility, however close you are in your relationship.

It's a fun idea, and it really captures the imagination. People love to know how well they're doing, and a quiz can turn deepening your love for each other into a game.

> **JOIN THE FUN**
>
> Come and join the fun on our Facebook page–there's even a quiz like the ones we used to get to know each other better.
>
> www.facebook.com/howmyhusbandkeepsmehappy/

Make the Effort

Communication helps. A lot of what you'll read about in this book is about learning to communicate on a much deeper level. But communication isn't enough.

Early on, Evan realized that if we were going to survive the challenges our schedules were putting on the relationship, he was going to have to show that he was 100% committed to making it work.

> **EVAN:** One weekend I came up to visit Karen as usual, but I arrived with groceries and fire logs. They were simple things—not what people traditionally think of as "romantic"—but I wanted to show that I was going to be a very good support mechanism for her and that I was playing for keeps.
>
> I also wanted to show her that there are nice guys out there who want more out of life. This

> relationship wasn't just about sex: I wanted a partner, somebody I could care about and love, and who would be a mother figure to my son.

There's always room for romantic gestures as well, of course, and those don't have to be expensive. A lot of people equate romance with how much you spend on something, when in fact, it's about how much thought you put into it.

On another weekend visit, Evan turned up with 30 bottles of wine (we didn't get through them all that weekend, before you ask!) There was a local winery where you could go and make your own wine. They would look after it while it fermented, and then you went and bottled it. The price was right, and it was handmade—and that's what counts.

Compatibility Counts

One of the great things about meeting on eHarmony was the amount of effort the site puts into helping you figure out whether you're compatible with a potential partner.

> **KAREN:** I'd been on a couple of other dating sites before eHarmony, but it didn't go well.

Guys would get upset over the tiniest things: it was no wonder they were single!

One time, I typed "Hi" to a guy in the chat box to start a conversation. He didn't reply, so I moved off his profile and started to look at who else was on the site. Half an hour later, he invited me to chat. It took me a minute to find his profile again and scan it quickly so I'd have something to talk to him about.

Suddenly, it disappeared. The last I saw from him was a message saying "You took too long to answer me" and an emoticon of a black cat (for bad luck), then he blocked me. So because I was too slow for his liking, he blocked me and cursed me. My only thought was "well, I understand why *you're* still single."

Another time, I was chatting with someone on a site, and we discovered that we lived quite close to each other. Since we were actually in the same city, it at least had the potential to go somewhere. Then he asked me if I'd dated anyone from the site, and I said that I had been in a two-year relationship, but it just didn't work out in the end. That was it: the guy cut me off and never chatted to me again.

> After experiences like those, I was *so* glad Evan was rational and nice, and that we are compatible.

As we both had sons from our previous marriages, a major aspect of "compatibility" for both of us was that our partner accepted our son and loved them as if he were their own son. More and more families these days are 'blended' families. More and more people are on their second (or even later) marriage. And that acceptance of "the whole package" is critical.

Often, when you're a single parent, you meet someone, and as soon as they find out that you have a child, it turns them off.

> **KAREN:** At our first social event together, someone said to Evan, "You know she has a kid, right?" As though it was some kind of flaw and he should run away while he still could.
>
> **EVAN:** In fact, of course, it was one of the things that had attracted me to her. One of the lines on my profile was that the person needed "to accept me and my son as a package," and Karen had a very similar line on hers. In fact, she listed it as one of her "deal breakers"!

For us, the eHarmony compatibility test was a major step in realizing what would make us good together, but what about couples who aren't on a dating site and can't take a test? What about couples who are already together?

Even without the test and the matching process, the clues were there for us. We share the same point of view on many things. We agree on things—large and small—and we see the world the same way. You could say we are "like-minded." That doesn't take a test to discover: you just have to talk—and listen—to each other.

In the film Jerry Maguire, there's a famous scene where the sports agent Jerry (played by Tom Cruise) tells his wife Dorothy, "You complete me." That's how it is for us: we complete each other. We each bring something to the relationship that the other is missing.

We had also both come from first marriages to people we weren't compatible with. Divorce is not fun. It's not good for anyone involved. And neither of us wanted to get married again and potentially expose ourselves—and our sons—to the whole ordeal again. But you have to take a leap of faith when the right relationship is in front of you.

We both wanted committed partners; faithful partners; partners who were on the same wavelength as us. We just hadn't planned to get married again. But then that, too, was just another way in which we were alike!

Focus on what matters

Let's face it, guys like to be "economical" and efficient: they want the biggest impact from the smallest effort.

Some couples struggle to keep their relationship fresh and alive because the husband keeps trying different things to try to please his wife but misses the mark. Eventually, it all starts to seem like hard work, and he stops trying.

There's a simple answer to that, and it's a word that keeps coming up in this book.

Listen

That's as important for the wife as for the husband. It's just that wives tend to be better at it.

Listen to your partner, and you'll know what's important to them. Then, when you're wondering what to do, focus on those things, and you'll always get it right.

Music is something else that binds us closer. We both grew up in the 70s, and we both love the music from that decade. A few weeks into our relationship, Evan sent one of his 4 a.m. emails. It said, simply, "Here's a song for you. It really touched my heart," and there was a link to a video.

The song was *Wildfire*.

> **EVAN:** I chose the song because it's about a girl and her horse. I knew that Karen's father was a horse trainer, so horses were a big part of her family's life growing up.
>
> **KAREN:** Ironically, cats are my favorite animal. But horses are the most beautiful animals, to my mind, so it worked. No-one had ever done anything like that before. It's more common now—and much easier—but then it was just sweet that he had taken something that was part of my life and he had thought to do that.

What's it all about?

For Evan, this is about much more than keeping the relationship fresh. It's about treating it as something sacred; something that is to be cherished and nurtured and protected.

> **EVAN:** I don't let anything harm our relationship. I don't let anything come between us. When I'm wrong, I'll admit I'm wrong, and Karen will do the same. Neither of us will ever go to bed angry. Life is way too short, and I've seen too many divorces, too many broken families. I'm in a happy place, and I want to stay there.

We have seen relationships where the man will put in a lot of effort at the beginning while they're dating, but once they get married or move in together, the effort stops. Men don't seem to understand that women really appreciate even the little things. It means a lot to them.

It's like keeping a car on the road. You maintain it. You go for the oil changes, and you get it serviced. You put gas in the tank, and you don't let it run on empty. All of that is much easier—and much cheaper—than letting it break down and being faced with a huge bill to get it fixed and back on the road.

Relationships are the same: you don't let your relationship run on empty, because it's not going to go very far.

Or you can think of it this way: do you want your wife to be happy or cranky?

Many husbands grew up seeing the way their parents' marriage worked (or didn't), and they try to run their own marriage the same way. But the world has changed. Almost all women work now, so they've got work to do and kids to take care of and a house to keep running.

Women don't want to be cranky and hard to be around. They get overwhelmed. That's why they get cranky: because they are tired and stressed and overwhelmed. The crankiness is a cry for help.

Evan often says, "happy wife, happy life." He truly believes that, because of everything he gets from Karen in return: intimacy, laughter, connection and full commitment.

Keeping your wife happy is a good way to keep your life happy, which is a great way to lead into the next chapter. But before we go to that, at the end of each chapter you'll find some questions to get you to reflect on your relationship and some tips and ideas to help you act on what we talk about in the chapter. The questions will only take a few moments to answer, and you can work on them together.

Rating

On a scale of 1-10, how good are you at keeping your relationship feeling fresh and exciting?

Question

What are some ways you could recapture how you felt about each other when you first got together?

Making this work

So, how can a couple get into this mindset and start working on keeping their relationship fresh?

- Find fun and different ways to communicate. An easy start is a text. Something that shows that you are thinking about your partner. Leave notes for each other around the house with a short, loving message. If you can't think what to say, get a preprinted pad of them—it's the thought that counts!

- Look out for something—a picture, a song, some little gift—that relates to something that's meaningful to your partner and give it to them. Gifts aren't just for birthdays and holidays.

- Create a little quiz that you can each take and then compare your answers afterward. Write the questions together: what's your favorite color? Your favorite TV show? Who's your favorite singer? The questions can literally be about anything: just remember to keep it fun and lighthearted. It's about opening up to each other and sharing the little things, because that makes it easier to open up and share the big things.

- Talk. Talk about the things that matter to you. Talk about what's happening in the world or in your lives. Find out all the things you have in common, and also the things that are different for each of you.

- However long you've been together, look for ways to show that you're committed to each other and to making the relationship work.

Chapter 2

Happy Wife, Happy Life

Right on cue, the doorbell rang. Karen tried not to rush down the hall to the door: she didn't want to seem overly keen and scare Evan away.

As she opened the door, she saw Evan on the doorstep, his breath forming clouds of vapor in the cold evening air. She went to hug him, and that was when she noticed that his hands were full. "I didn't want to turn up empty handed," he said, holding out two bags of groceries. "There's a box of fire logs in the car, too!"

Evan's focus is on keeping the energy in our relationship as if we were still dating. He is constantly looking for ways to keep things alive. One of the ways he does that is by helping with chores around the house.

Modern life has changed, as we said earlier in the book. The life our parents' generation had is very different from the life of most couples today. For them, a wife was a wife and mother first and foremost, and therefore men grew up seeing their mothers as the person who did everything around the house and their father as the one who went to work and then came back home and watched football, drank beer, and so on. Today, a wife is often faced with being a joint breadwinner and at the same time the homemaker.

That can put a lot of pressure and stress on her, and that in turn puts a lot of stress and strain on the relationship.

> **KAREN:** My dad was self-employed, so he worked seven days a week. My mother worked sporadically, but she was mostly a homemaker: she did a lot for all of us, including us kids. Maybe that's why I'm really enjoying having someone in my life who participates in my life and enjoys being helpful.
>
> Their situation was different: my father was lost in the kitchen. It's not that he didn't care. He was busy working every day, and she was always there to take care of things. They had different duties, and it worked for them.

Dad trained and raced horses. He would be up at 5 a.m. to be on the farm at 6 a.m., and sometimes he would work through to the evening.

That changed when my mother was diagnosed with cancer. When she started treatment, she couldn't do everything that she had been doing, so she showed him how to cook and do the laundry. Up until that time, he was always working, and she was always taking care of us, so he had never needed to learn. By the end, though, we would go over there, and he would be in the kitchen: he knew what he was doing, and he was helping to cook the meals.

One day I found him washing the dishes. I said, "Dad, why are you washing the dishes, you have a dishwasher right there?" He replied, "I like it, it relaxes me." I thought to myself, *who are you, and what have you done with my father?*

A year after my mother passed away, my dad met Nancy, and they live together now. He still helps in the kitchen, and he even makes breakfast for us when we go over.

Apart from a few years after Ryan was born, Karen has always been in full-time work and balanced that with being a mother and a wife. Once Ryan started school, she went back to work, but within a year found herself starting a new life as a working single mother.

> **KAREN:** I can't even imagine going through that without at least having a job and some income of my own. We live in an older house, and if something needed to be done on it, I was the one who had to do it or get it done. If Ryan was sick, my mom would come over to look after him while I was out at work, but even so, it got to the point where I desperately needed help. I remember thinking, *This is just too much! Everything needs to get done, and it all has to get done by me!*

When Evan turned up with groceries and fire logs, it was a nice surprise—after all, who doesn't appreciate food? But to Evan, it was second nature.

> **EVAN:** I get that trait from my mother. She never went anywhere without bringing something—that was just how I was brought up. So I wasn't going to come here and eat Karen's food without making some sort of contribution.

Now that we're married, we still like to go shopping together on the weekend and discover new foods.

There's a big difference in a relationship when the husband helps out around the house and when they don't. Evan helps around the house a lot: not just the maintenance, but cooking and vacuuming.

> **EVAN:** It's another trait that I get from my mother. Growing up, my siblings and I did the dishes every day; we cleaned the house; we cut the grass; we shoveled the driveways regularly. My mother was a very good cook, and we helped out in the kitchen. It wasn't that it was expected: we just did it. We could see how hard our mother was working and we wanted to help. We had our own snow route, so ours was always the first house to get shoveled, and we would fight over who was going to shovel first. I relish those times now because they made me who I am today.
>
> **KAREN:** The only thing he seems to struggle with is the laundry: he can do it, but putting it away is an event on its own.
>
> When I fold the laundry, I sit on a stool and fold it as I take it out of the dryer. I take out all the shirts and fold them, then I do all the

> pants, and so on. Everything ends up organized in the basket.
>
> When Evan folds the laundry, how it comes out of the dryer is how it goes in the basket: one sock, then a pair of underwear, then another sock…
>
> Then he'll hang up things that don't need to be hung up or put them away in the wrong drawer, so getting dressed turns into a bizarre game of hide-and-seek.

Son and Dad Picnic Night.

When Evan was a single dad, he would get to see Aidan every other weekend. He would pick him up, and on the way home, the first stop would be the grocery store to stock up on dill pickles, cherry tomatoes, carrots, celery, pepperettes, mini bagels and potato chips: everything needed for a son and dad picnic night.

When they got home, all the food would go into bowls on the table, then Aidan would pick a movie and put it in the player, and for two hours it was just father-and-son time.

Evan would drink beer, and Aidan would drink ginger beer. Or Evan would have wine and Aidan would have grape juice: Evan always picked something that would make Aidan feel like he was just like dad.

When we first met, a second picnic night was added, on the Fridays when Evan didn't have Aidan. It was Karen and Evan Picnic Night. We would have wine and *hors d'oeuvres*, and we'd sit and watch Dateline together, or a murder mystery.

We still do it, every Friday. Date night doesn't have to be about spending lots of money on a fancy restaurant. It can be a few foods you both enjoy, a bottle of something you'll both like, and a TV program or a movie in front of the fire.

In the summer, we go out on the deck and sit, watching the sun go down. We've created a little sanctuary with a fountain, and lights all around.

> **EVAN:** Living in the city, I'd never watched a sunset until I met Karen. The first one I ever saw was on our back deck. Karen's mother had just been diagnosed with her second bout of cancer and the family all got together for a barbecue. We were all sitting on the deck, watching this huge ball of fire sink below the horizon. I suddenly realized that it was

> something we all take for granted, but here was a woman whose life was ending and who wouldn't see many more of those, so we started watching a lot of sunsets in the backyard. Whenever I see a sunset now, I think of Karen's mom.

Karen sometimes thinks that her mom manifested Evan for her. She would say, "I'm not dying while you're single. I'm going to get you married before I die." She wanted peace of mind, knowing that Karen had a kind partner in her life. In fact, it was she who suggested Karen try eHarmony. And she was also the reason why we both decided to get married, even though we'd both told ourselves we would never get married again.

> **KAREN:** Evan and I were visiting my parents when the phone rang. My mother answered it, and after chatting for a short while, she said, "I'll call you back later. My daughter and son-in-law are here visiting."
>
> Evan and I looked at each other, and I jokingly said "I don't remember getting married. Do you?"

My mother explained that she felt we were too old to be referred to as "boyfriend and girlfriend."

A few months later, we were at my parents' house, and the phone rang again. This time, when my mother explained why she had to go, she said, "My daughter and her husband are here, so I'll call you back tomorrow."

We drove home in silence, both deep in thought. We were both thinking the same thing, and in the end, I broke the silence. "You know, we could make a dying woman's wish come true."

Without hesitation, Evan replied, "Let's make it happen."

EVAN: As one of our last family vacations before she died, Karen's mom arranged to rent a cottage at Sherkston Shores for a week.

One afternoon, I asked Karen to take her mom and the two boys for a ride on the golf cart because I wanted to talk to her dad alone. After they had left, I offered Garth a beer and said, "I want to run something by you."

Garth replied, "Oh, what would that be?"

> "I have been putting some thought into Karen and I getting married," I said. "What do you think of that?"
>
> Garth looked at me with a smile and said, "I think that would be a very good idea."
>
> I was glad to hear it. Maybe I'm old fashioned, but I wanted his blessing.

Why this matters

Why is it so important for a husband to keep their wife happy (and for a wife to keep her husband happy!) apart from the obvious—that if they're unhappy, they will wander off?

Simply put, life is too short.

We both learned from our first marriage—and divorce—that life is short, and you have to make the most of what you have. Neither of us wants to go through anything like that again, so it's in our interest to keep each other happy.

It's much easier to keep a marriage going well than it is to fix a marriage that is broken. It's much easier to just start putting effort into your relationship and make it work. Divorce was ten times worse than either of us thought it was going to be: it's expensive, stressful, and just plain awful.

Marriage is all about building a future together, building equity, building a family. Divorce is the complete opposite: it is all about tearing it down and dividing it. It's undoing what you were trying to do all those years.

"Happy Wife, Happy Life" is not a new idea, and although it's one of Evan's catchphrases, he didn't invent it. You see and hear it everywhere, so you have to wonder why it is that not all men sign up to it and think that way.

We are each other's rock and each other's foundation. That is how you have to think of your partner. Of course, support has to go both ways.

> **EVAN:** I know I can always depend on Karen. One weekend, I'd been visiting my aunt in Scarborough, which is about 70 miles from us, and I left some tools there. I thought I could pick them up next time I visited, but the following weekend I needed them here, and I had a work event to attend. I ran out of time, so Karen drove over to pick them up for me.
>
> Another time we had my son Aidan visiting us, and I had to take him back to my ex-wife's,

> which is about 50 miles from us. I was exhausted, so I told Karen I was taking a nap on the couch, and I'd take Aidan back when I woke up. Well, when I did wake up the house was silent and in darkness. Karen had taken him back for me so I could rest.

We both find that kind of thing just "natural." It shouldn't be an effort to help your partner out. And it shouldn't be that hard to find opportunities to help out. We all need help with a thousand little things each day. All you need to do is be on the lookout for ways to make your partner's life easier.

Some friends of ours are no longer together because the husband wouldn't do anything for his wife. It was astonishing to watch from outside. If "her" car broke down, he wouldn't fix it. Evan was a car mechanic when he was younger, so he offered to help one time, and the husband wouldn't pay for the parts. It was "her" car so she should pay for the parts. Things like that are a warning sign. It's not just about the principle, it's about what marriage means to those two people. If a marriage isn't a support structure where both sides can rely on and can be relied upon by each other then what's the point?

So, let's assume that you're reading this book because you want to make your relationship better. How can you start thinking this way?

Rating

On a scale of 1-10, how sensitive are you to noticing when your partner is stressed or overwhelmed?

Question

How would your relationship be different if both of you felt more relaxed and under less pressure?

Making this work

- You don't need to reinvent the wheel. It can start with something as simple as taking the time to do something your partner enjoys. We'll sit and watch a hockey game together because it's something that is important to Evan

- If your partner looks stressed, have a conversation. Ask if there is anything you can do to help, or if they want to talk about what's going on.

- Listen. You'll pick up a lot listening to what's actually being said and—just as importantly—what isn't being said, and if you're not listening, you'll miss the SOS.

- If you're home before your partner, meet them at the door with a drink (hot, cold alcoholic or non-alcoholic—whichever they prefer!) and a hug. Or run a bubble bath ready for when they get home. If your partner is home before you, stop at the coffee shop and pick up a couple of drinks to take home.

- Bring your partner a coffee in bed first thing in the morning.

- Ask if there are any chores your partner would like help with.

Chapter 3

Show Them You Care

Karen flicked on the lights as she came through the front door. Something was different. It took a moment to register, and then she figured it out. The light was different. That was when she spotted the pile of lightbulbs on the table and Evan's note. "I know you couldn't afford to swap all your old bulbs for LEDs, so I switched them for you. You also have new smoke detectors. Love, Evan oxo"

We were still dating when Evan carried out the Great Lightbulb Swap. Life as a single mother was challenging, and Evan knew that. He also knew that LED light bulbs for the whole house weren't in the budget, but Karen needed it! Ryan had a habit of turning on lights and leaving them on after he left the room, so switching from 60W incandescent bulbs to 4W LEDs was a huge saving.

LED bulbs were selling for $6-$8 back then, so changing all the bulbs came to $150. Karen needed the $150 to keep the lights on, so it wouldn't have happened without Evan.

Nowadays, all the lights—inside the house and outside—are LED. Even the Christmas lights and Halloween lights are LED. So, Evan's pet name is 'Captain LED' (at least, that's the one we can put in this book!).

> **KAREN:** When I realized what he'd done, I was speechless. It was pretty clear he was in this for the long-haul. He was committed, and this wasn't going to be just a couple of dates with me and then a couple of dates with somebody else. Even in his free time, he was putting his energy into trying to make a relationship work with me.

The way to think of it is as an investment. You invest in your marriage or relationship today, knowing that you'll reap the benefits in the future.

Of course, when you're dating, buying light bulbs is extraordinary. When you're married, it's just what you do. So you need to switch.

Making things better

A few years ago, Evan had a vision for the back yard. It didn't look great, and we'd been saying that we wanted somewhere that would be a little corner of calm and beauty just for us. In the end, we didn't spend a lot of money on it, but it took effort, and by the time he was done, the difference from what we had before he started to what he created was night and day.

He had to take out a lot of shrubs and do a lot of landscaping. We used some of our wedding money to buy an arbor, and he put that in too. Evan was given several hundred edge stones for free, so he and Aidan used them to edge the perimeter of the yard.

> **KAREN:** Evan did most of the work while I was out for the day. When I came back, I was speechless and almost in tears. I never dreamt the backyard could look so good.

It took the rest of the summer to finish the yard, with new plants being added every week. We've also added new lights, a swing, and a fountain. It was another way for Evan to show that he was committed; that the two of us could build this into something pretty special.

EVAN: Aidan was a big help with the project: picking stones for the rock garden (some of them weighed as much as 150 pounds!), and finding odd and wonderful plants. It was a real father-and-son work of art when it was finished.

Sirius-ly?

EVAN: Karen's car came with a free three-month trial subscription to a digital radio service called Sirius. Her favorite station was the Elvis channel—it was on every time she got in the car.

When the notifications started to come through to say the trial was expiring, Karen wanted to renew it, but she couldn't find any details about how much it would cost, so she let it lapse.

When I got a new car some time later, it came with a free Sirius trial too. I'd only had it a month when they started to call me about a special promotional rate they had for "preferred customers."

> It wasn't much use to me because I still had a few months to run on my free trial, but only the day before Karen had been saying how much she wished she still had Sirius. She was missing The King!
>
> That little side note had been stored away in my mind, so when I got the call, my first thought was to ask if they could give Karen the special rate instead. Like any good salesperson, the service representative told me he had to check with his manager, but of course, he came back a few moments later, and the deal was done. The King was back!

Why this matters

Marriage is an investment. Not of money, but of time, effort and above all an emotional investment. It's something that both of you have to put in, and both of you reap the benefits from that investment over time.

It's like a savings account: you've got to keep adding to it to see it grow, and as the years go by you get more and more out of it.

What matters just as much, though, is quality. You get out what you put in. Evan likes to sum it up as "quality in, quality out." Do the small things in a marriage to get the big things out of it: little hinges swing big doors.

Ultimately, it comes down to respect; being appreciated and valued in a relationship. Those are all important.

> **KAREN:** One of the ways my mother showed my father how much she cared was through food. She was a great believer in the old saying that the way to a man's heart is through his stomach.
>
> We used to spend a lot of time cooking together—Evan loves to cook—but that changed after I started a new job. Sometimes, I have to be away at conferences for two or three days at a time. Other times, even though I'm working more locally, I may be out into the evening. So we end up having takeout more than we used to.
>
> **EVAN:** Karen will call from wherever she is and say, "I'm just leaving. Should I pick something up?" If she's away, she'll call from her hotel room, and we'll just talk about what has been happening that day.

The key is that we just communicate and share. And if something matters to one of us, then it matters to both of us.

Evan's mother is 75 this year, and he hadn't been to New Brunswick to visit her for 5 years, even though she has come out to Ontario many times to visit family.

> **EVAN:** This year I had three weeks of vacation due, so I decided it was time to head out east. Karen had never spent any one-on-one time with my mother because whenever she comes out here, there's always lots to do like seeing family and friends. I also knew that mom would have been storing up a 'sonny do' list for me: she knows that I'm handy, and she always has things to be done around the house. So we drove down. Karen dreaded the thought of the 15-hour drive, but she agreed to do it because she knew it was important to me and she wanted to spend time with her mother-in-law on her birthday.

Rating

On a scale of 1-10, how good are you at spotting things to do that will please your partner without having to be asked?

Question

What are some of the things you could do right now for your partner that you know would bring a smile to their face?

Making this work

- Remember what it was that attracted you to each other in the first place. Talk about it and build on it.

- Don't assume that your partner knows how much you love them: show them, tell them, and hold them.

- Ask your partner what you can do to show your love. Have a conversation, do a check-in and see.

- Set one night aside as date night. It doesn't have to be expensive: it's about the thought you put in, not how much you spend. Light some candles, have some drinks, set out some snacks, and watch a good movie.

Chapter 4

Listen (And Prove It)

We talked about our life dreams right from the start. We did that because we didn't want to get into a relationship and then discover, six months in, that we were headed in different directions. Sharing our goals and ideas was just another way of showing that we are in this for the long haul.

It's important for a couple to have shared dreams. Of course, they each have to have their own dreams and goals, but there has to be something that both of you are working towards together. Without that, it is too easy for both partners to either drift along, living separate lives or in the worst case end up pulling apart as they each chase conflicting dreams.

eHarmony made it easier for us because there were questions that asked us to specify what we wanted in life and in a partner. The problem is, life doesn't come with a questionnaire, so most couples are in the dark, so you have to start having that conversation yourselves, and then keep it going.

Even now, ten years in, we still talk about our dreams and aspirations, and set them together. Our shared goals revolve around time, money and freedom. We look around and see ordinary people making extraordinary money, and we ask ourselves, "How can we do that?"

The funny thing is, the bigger our dreams have gotten, the better we have become at manifesting. Even the book you're reading now is something that we manifested together.

Listen to the small stuff, too

> **KAREN:** Evan thinks he has a decoder ring for how I am feeling and what I am thinking. For the most part, I think he might be right: in the past, I have been surprised by how quickly he notices when I am upset about something, even when I am trying really hard to hide it!

Listening isn't just about being able to share the 'big' stuff. We all need someone who will listen to us when we want to talk about day-to-day stuff, too; it's a basic human need for many people. Without it, we can feel isolated and alone, without support: the exact opposite of what a loving relationship is supposed to be like.

Sometimes, the greatest thing you can do for your partner is to just sit and listen, even though there may be something else vying for your attention. But you have to be listening, not just pretending to listen!

> **EVAN:** When Karen was going through a difficult time, she would need to vent almost daily for the best part of twenty minutes.
>
> During those twenty minutes, I would just sit and nod. If she asked me a direct question, I would reply, but otherwise, I would just let her get stuff off her chest. She didn't want me to try and fix the problem; just listen to it.

That's difficult for most husbands: men tend to be problem solvers. You give them a problem, and their natural instinct is to come up with a solution. Or rather, you give them half the problem, and they try to solve it. That can drive their wife crazy, especially if what they wanted was someone to just listen to them.

The challenge is to know which kind of conversation you're in: a vent or a brainstorm. That's where you need to listen. Your partner will give you clues, and over time you'll learn what they are. It could be the words they use, a particular tone of voice or a change in the speed they talk at. You can figure it out if you take the time to listen.

> **KAREN:** If I'm frustrated about a situation, he knows I just need to vent for a few minutes, because something has me worked up, and I just need to get it out. I just think if I can talk to someone, it'll make me feel better.
>
> Before I met Evan, I was dating someone else. One day, he called me as I was driving home and asked, "How was your day?"
>
> That day, a few things had happened that were quite frustrating. I started to tell him, but after a few minutes, I realized he wasn't even listening, and then I could tell he was annoyed because I'd shared it with him and asked his opinion.
>
> I just thought, *Really? You asked me how my day was, so I told you. There was something that happened that upset me, and I was just letting you know because you asked me. Thanks for being totally unsupportive!*

This is not rocket science: you just have to listen. You may see the mouth moving, but if you're not processing those words, there is no communication.

The only thing we don't see eye-to-eye on is hockey: the Toronto Maple Leafs and the Montreal Canadiens. But even there, Evan is used to being in the minority as the only Canadiens fan on a street of Maple Leafs fans.

It takes two to tango

We were having dinner at a local restaurant, and there was a flyer on the table about Argentine tango lessons, so we picked it up.

> **EVAN:** It was a little before our wedding, and Karen had been worrying about our first dance. Karen loves dancing, but we didn't know anything about tango. Still, I knew she wanted some practice before our first dance, so we signed up for the lessons. Neither of us had ever done any tango before, and we didn't understand what we were getting ourselves into! We both soon realized we were in over our heads, but we stuck to it and finished all the lessons.

In the end, it all worked out. We winged it on the dance floor at our wedding. The song we chose was "History in the Making" by Darius Rucker, and Evan sang the words as we danced.

Sink your teeth into the problem

They say that a problem shared is a problem halved. Even something that seems inconsequential to you can be a big deal to your partner, so helping them to solve it can bring you closer together.

> Evan almost walked past the store. In the last few hours, he had tried 13 different drugstores, beauty stores, gift stores, departments stores: you name a store he'd been into it. Even as he walked up to the cash desk, he knew what the answer would be.
>
> "I am here on a noble quest. My wife has sent me looking for one of these. Do you have one?"
>
> The shop owner picked the item up and looked at it carefully. "No."
>
> "Do you know where I can get one?"
>
> "No. But if you find one, I'll buy a dozen!"
>
> You see, Karen has a problem. It's a very personal problem. Not one she likes to talk

about in public. But, hey, this book is all about openness and communication, right?

OK, here it is: in winter, when the weather is really cold and dry, her hair gets supercharged with static and fluffs up into a giant hairball. She looks like a gremlin, and plastic combs just make it worse.

She's only ever found one fix: an untreated wooden comb that she picked up at a store in Toronto many years ago.

And then, one day, disaster struck. A relative was visiting and made a puddle on the bathroom counter (not that kind of puddle; just water!). After a day soaking, the wood warped, and the next time Karen tried to use it, it snapped into pieces.

You'd think replacing it would be simple. But no, they were nowhere to be found.

Evan knew it mattered to Karen, so it got stored "up there" for later:

☐ *Buy comb for Karen*

And so here he was, trying every mall and specialty store in town, with no success. (He eventually found one on Ebay!)

So many people struggle to come up with a gift idea for their partner, whether for Christmas or a birthday or just as a surprise to say "I love you and I care." And yet the clues are there, in the things they say and do every single day.

All you have to do is be willing to listen and then store it away for when it's needed. When you do that, you avoid buying your special someone a gift that they didn't want and surprise them with something they will truly appreciate. That pays off in spades in a relationship, especially if you're doing it as a matter of course.

> **EVAN:** Put thought into gifts. I would never just give Karen a gift card from a tool and hardware store (even though it's something I would appreciate for myself!). Karen would much rather get a gift certificate for a spa—she even wants me to do a couples package with her one day. I'll keep you posted!

Now you might think all of this is high maintenance. It isn't. This is about consistently doing little things that add up, not just making one extravagant gesture once in a blue moon. It's about finding ways to make the person you love happy.

The Payoff

And in case you're wondering, the payoff for Evan came shortly after.

> **KAREN:** Evan was driving an old 1993 Ford Ranger, and it was on its last legs. He's a great mechanic, so he was keeping it on the road, but it really was on life support. We had a newer car, too, but he insisted that I have that and he'd keep driving the truck, mostly because he knew that if the truck broke down while he was driving it, he would probably be able to get it home, but if it happened to me, I'd be stranded.
>
> Then one day he came up to me. "I want to buy a motorcycle. What do you think?"

We'll come back to this later when we talk about Respect, Trust, and Loyalty. It's something we always do: when there's a big decision, even if it sounds like something that's really just for one of us, we discuss it together. As it happens, that decision did affect both of us. Driving to work and back each day was a 30-mile round trip. In the truck, he was spending $50 a week on gas. With the bike that has gone down to $10 a week.

So Evan spent $10 on a comb and got to spend $5,000 on a new bike. Plus the leathers and the safety gear and everything else that goes with owning a new bike. Not a bad deal!

Why this matters

We shouldn't need to say why listening matters, but just in case...

It proves that you care and what that other person wants or is talking about, matters to you. When your partner knows they are being listened to, they feel valued and respected. If you aren't taking the time to listen and care, there might be somebody else who comes along that does take the time to listen to them. They go to work, and there's a co-worker who is willing to lend an ear or seems more interested in what they have to say, and that leads to coffee, and who knows where that could lead!

Listening just takes a little of your time and effort. When you are in a new relationship, there is a lot to talk about. It might seem trivial to you, but you need to keep that dialog going even when the relationship isn't new anymore.

Rating

On a scale of 1-10, how good are you at listening actively to what your partner is saying?

Question

Make a list of some of the things that your partner has said in passing would please them: something they want, or something they would like done and can't do for themselves.

Making this work

- When your partner is talking to you, make a point of putting aside anything else you were doing. Don't multitask. That means turning off your laptop, putting down your phone and maybe even turning off the TV.

- When you hear something that is an opportunity to take action, follow up on it.

Chapter 5

Let The World Know How Much You Love Her

A lot of this book is about telling your partner how much you love them, but we also believe in telling the world in general how much in love you are. With so many relationships in turmoil, we believe it's important to set an example to your friends and family. Also, when you've been through turbulent relationships, as both of us have, the people close to you—friends, parents, siblings—worry. Being open and demonstrative about your feelings is a good way to reduce their worry.

> **EVAN:** My mother still lives out east, and even though I'm 54, she still thinks of me as her little boy. She saw me through the turmoil of my first marriage, and she knows I've been given a second chance, so it's important for her to know that I'm happy and my life is fulfilled. My sister also sees it. She said to me once, "I

knew you guys were going to be big; I just didn't know how big."

I feel empowered when I'm around Karen because I know she is the person I'm going home with, the person I go to sleep next to, and the person I wake up next to.

We often joke that we "like breathing the same air": if we're at home, we'll find that we end up in the same room, whatever we are doing. That's how much I'm connected, and the word I keep using is *magic*.

Now, we're not saying that we are wandering around town breaking into public displays of affection every few feet. Often, our demonstrations will just consist of goofing off and being silly. We might be walking through the mall, and suddenly Evan will jump up onto the catwalk and do a little dance. It's about finding ways to make each other laugh and not being embarrassed to do it in public. Most importantly, it's a continuation of how we are around the house. It's not a show that we are putting on for the benefit of other people: it's how we are whether other people are around or not. If anything, we have to tone things down in public!

Equally important, it's not just about reassuring other people: there's a big emotional payoff for both of us too.

> **EVAN:** When I'm walking down the street holding Karen's hand, it's electric. I see her sparkle because she's happy and I'm with her. That brightens my day. And it's a loop: I feed off of her emotion, as she feeds off of mine. So, if she sees me happy, she's happy; when I see her happy, I'm happy. It's self-sustaining. I wouldn't do something that is going to make her unhappy or cry; it's just not in me.

But what are we going to tell the kids?

Both of us had been married before, and both of us had children from that earlier marriage. It's a situation that more and more couples find themselves in, and it brings with it the question of how to tell those children that you are in a new relationship.

For Evan, it was easy. His son had already said he was ready for him to meet someone. So all Evan had to say was, "I have somebody that I want you to meet, and she has a son named Ryan."

In contrast, Ryan didn't get much notice that there was someone new in his mother's life. He was playing around in the family room.

> **KAREN:** He had the cushions off, making a fort, and I told him that there was somebody coming over that I wanted him to meet.

At that point, we had been dating for six weeks, and it felt like the right time. We both knew we were in this for the long term. More importantly, it was hard trying to fit dating in around the kids!

Telling other people was a harder decision, and we kept it secret for a while. Evan's brother has a habit of "telling it like it is," and sometimes gives Evan advice he doesn't want. It's one of his best qualities, because you know you'll get a straight answer, but Evan knew he'd be cautious: as we said above, the people nearest to you want to protect you, especially if they've seen you get burned before.

In fact, we needn't have been worried. Evan's brother and his wife were the first members of our extended families to invite us over for dinner when we finally "went public."

Our first public appearance together was Evan's company party the Christmas after we met. It was convenient because a lot of Evan's friends were there, along with his brother and sister-in-law, and the couple Evan was sharing a house with. Two weeks later, it was Evan's turn to be shown off to friends and co-workers at Karen's Christmas party!

Rating

On a scale of 1-10, how good are you at letting your partner know how you feel about them?

Question

What are some of the things you could do right now to demonstrate to your partner how much they mean to you?

Making this work

- Offer to look after the children so your partner can go out and do something fun for him/herself.

- Write a short note listing some of the things you love about your partner.

- Write them a love letter or a note.

- Cuddle.

Chapter 6

Evan's Story

At this point in the book, we want to take an aside from talking about our marriage and share how we got here. We didn't want to put this in the introduction because we didn't want this to be a book about dating, but rather about how to build on the relationship you already have. At the same time, we want to share our journey because it may be something you've been through, or maybe even something that you're going through right now.

As we've said before, this is Evan's second marriage. Indeed, this is the second marriage for both of us. If you've been married before, then you know that it can be tempting, even when you're settled into a good second marriage, to dwell on what went wrong with the first one. It's easy to fall into the trap of saying "I forgive her/him, but…"

Here's the thing. If you still think about what your last partner did wrong, then you haven't forgiven them.

And if you haven't forgiven them, and you just keep going over the old problems in your mind, it's toxic. Ultimately, they won't know you're still thinking about them, so it has no impact on their life. Where it does have an impact, however, is on your life and on your new relationship.

So, in this chapter, we're not going to pick apart why Evan's first marriage failed. Instead, we'll focus on how our relationship started, from his point of view.

> In many ways, the transition was an ordeal by fire. A seven-year ordeal, at that, however, sometimes you have to go through something really bad to get something really good.
>
> It took seven years to get divorced: one year more than we'd actually been married! So, understandably, I wasn't looking to jump into a new marriage. I wanted a stable relationship, but there was still too much pain associated with the idea of *marriage*.
>
> At first, I didn't date. I buried myself in work and my son.
>
> One of my first 'dates' was taking Aidan to the movies. Jim Carrey was starring in *How The Grinch Stole Christmas* and Aidan wanted to see it. When I got to the box office, the 8 p.m. and

10:15 p.m. showings were sold out. The only time I could get tickets was 12:15 a.m.!

By this point, Aidan, who was just 7 years old at the time, had tears streaming down his face. "Dad, I really want to see the Grinch!" he said. So I got tickets for the late movie. It was huge for him.

We also had Son and Dad Picnic night every time I had him, which was every other weekend. Friday night was something we did together that was special. We played table hockey, and if he did something well, he got an extra story. I could get him to do anything if I said "extra story at bedtime." He also loved going for a bike ride, because he knew that somewhere in the bike ride there was going to be ice cream.

And that was my life for two years after the divorce came through.

Then one summer we went up to Manitoulin Island in Northern Ontario. It's a beautiful, wild place, and it was probably the best holiday Aidan and I have ever had together. To this day, he still talks about it.

It rains up there, and a tent can get very claustrophobic if you have to sit in it staring at each other for too long, so the tent was strictly for sleeping. I set up a big area outside the tent covered with tarps; that way, when the weather was bad, we could sit outside and still do things. I also set up a kitchen tent for cooking. We had a fire, and we would sit and watch a movie or play games. It worked well, and Aidan loved it.

When we got back, all Aidan could talk about was how great the place was: the snakes and fossils and tree frogs he'd found, the stars he'd seen, and the wolves he'd heard howling. So we went back the second year, and I brought my brother with me with his two kids. Unfortunately, we discovered that none of them are natural campers. While they stuck with it, my brother didn't sleep too well, and his children didn't enjoy the experience as much as Aidan and I did.

On that same vacation, we decided to take a trip up to Science North in Sudbury, Ontario. Aidan spent the day walking through a giant model of a person's intestine, and he took a ride in a bush plane simulator: there were snakes around his feet, and he was getting sprayed with water. Needless to say, he loved it.

On the way back, though, he was silent, which was odd. He sat staring out of the van window for a long time, daydreaming, and then he turned to me and said, "Dad, when you meet someone, can you make sure they have some kids, so I have some step-brothers and sisters?"

I was dumbstruck. All I could think of to say was "OK," then Aidan made me promise!

He went back to staring out of the window for a couple of minutes and then he said, "Dad, can you do it soon?"

I knew at that point, he was ready for me to meet somebody. He always wanted a sibling, and that's why he loved being around my niece and nephew because it gave him companions. It threw me for a loop because I had no idea where to meet someone, and I was out of practice when it came to dating. I didn't want to meet someone in a bar, because you never know who you'll meet or whether they're married or not.

All my friends were married or in committed relationships. I was the odd one out in my social group, so hanging out with them wasn't going to help me meet someone either.

Then one night I was sitting at home watching TV, and an ad came on for eHarmony. It said something along the lines of, "Join eHarmony and find your life-long mate. Review your matches free this weekend."

I had just bought a computer, so I went on there. I was reading through some articles and helpful tips, and it said that you may not find true love at the start. It may take two or three times, and up to six months, so I thought *OK I'll join for 6 months.*

I spent about three hours completing my profile, and I put a lot of thought into my answers because I wanted it to work. There were no one-word answers.

When I hit enter, I had fourteen matches. I actually got scared at that point. I turned off the computer, and I didn't go back to it for a few days. Then curiosity got the better of me, and I logged in again.

Another suggestion I found on the site was to be open to looking for someone outside your immediate area, so I switched the search radius from 10 miles to 50 miles.

This time when I hit enter, I had 54 matches, and Karen was one of the 54. In the end, she was the only person I communicated with on eHarmony.

People ask me how I knew to get in touch with her. I'm not sure, but I think I was steered in that direction with a little magic.

I'd love to say that I saw her photo and fell instantly in love, but this isn't a fairy tale. It sounds nuts, but when I saw her picture, the first thing I noticed was that she was holding a cat. I'm a cat person, so that caught my attention. Then in her profile, she said she had a son and she didn't smoke. That was two more things that ticked all the right boxes. So I sent her a request to communicate, and within a day she had responded.

Back then, eHarmony's process only let you send standard questions at first, until you were both ready for what it called *open communication*. Karen asked me "What was the last book you read?"

I'm totally honest and transparent, so I answered: "I just bought a new car, so the last book I read was my 2007 Suzuki Swift manual."

She thought that was funny. It was an honest answer, but she thought it was clever; clever enough to continue reading my profile. When I told her later that I really did read my new car manual, she said she thought I was joking. She said, "But I thought men don't read manuals!"

Well, this one does. I've always read manuals and instructions. I figure I don't know everything, and maybe I can learn something.

We went into the dos and don'ts of what I wanted in a relationship: I sent her my list, and she sent me hers. I wanted a committed relationship with somebody who would accept my son and me as a package, and she had the same answer, almost word for word. So I knew we were both on the same wavelength.

I didn't want to get involved with someone for a few months and then have it fall apart. I couldn't put myself, or my son, through that hardship again. I didn't have the energy for it. Also, I wanted to have one side of Aidan's life that would always be stable. To this day, he knows that he can come to me and tell me anything. He knows that his father is his rock. If he screws up, I'll still call him a dumbass, but he also knows that I'll take care of him, support him and put him first.

One night, about three weeks in, I came home and saw that there was a new message for me on eHarmony. It was from Karen: "We should meet for a drink."

Now, this wasn't the way it was supposed to go. My understanding was that we should do two weeks of "open email communication" through their system, then a phone call. Of course, I'd done my checking: her Facebook profile had the same photo as on the site, so I knew she was a real person. But I was still cautious, and remember: at this point, we hadn't even talked on the phone!

Looking back it was hilarious. I honestly didn't know what to do. The eHarmony instructions were very exact.

I asked some of the girls at work, "The woman I've been chatting with on eHarmony wants to meet for a drink. What should I do?"

"They looked at me like I was nuts, "Go for a drink!"

At the time I was living with a friend, Chris, and his wife, so I asked Chris for a favor. I was meeting Karen at 8 p.m. on Saturday, and I asked him to call at 8:05 p.m. with an emergency. By then, I figured I'd know if things were going to go badly and I'd have a way to get out of it.

I turned up early, at 7:55 p.m., but Karen had beaten me there by ten minutes. When the greeter at the restaurant told me she was already there, I started to sweat and think about all the things that could go wrong.

Then I saw her for the first time. My immediate thought was *classy*. She was everything I'd hoped for and more, and her profile picture really didn't do her justice.

Needless to say, when Chris called I didn't answer my phone, even when Karen said, "I think your phone is ringing."

For the next 90 minutes, I talked almost non-stop while she ate her nachos and my steak sandwich went cold. I told her about my son, and she told me about hers (when she could get a word in). We were both very committed to our families, which pleased me. I told her about my work, and she told me about hers. The one thing neither of us talked about was our exes—which apparently was a huge relief for Karen, compared to other dates she had been on.

Another thing that set me apart from other dates she'd had—and this just astonishes me—is that I picked up the tab for both of us. To me, it was natural, but it seems not all men think that way.

At the end, I said, "This has been great fun, I'd like to do it again." Luckily for me, she hadn't been put off by my chattering, and she said yes.

We'd actually forgotten to swap phone numbers in all the excitement, so for the next two weeks, we carried on communicating through eHarmony.

For our second date, we went to The Keg Steakhouse and Bar, and this time Karen insisted on paying half. Then we went bowling. Now, I'm pretty competitive, so I wasn't going to let her win, even if it cost me a third date!

Because of my schedule and the timing of our times with our children, we only saw each other alternate weekends, so we decided after just four dates that we needed to introduce the boys to each other. Otherwise, it was going to take forever!

We arranged to all meet up for a day on a farm in Milton, Ontario.

At first, the boys were bashful around each other. They are actually two totally different personalities. But by the end of two hours, they were checking out girls together, going for hay rides and exploring mazes like they'd always been siblings. It was magical for us to see them like that.

In January 2008—we'd been dating for three months—my boss dropped a bombshell. He needed me to switch to the weekend shift. I'd fought for seven years to get my weekends with my son, and my boss knew it was non-negotiable for me. So I handed in my notice, saying I'd stay until they found a replacement.

It took five months for the company to hire someone. In that time I relied heavily on my support network. Either the couple I was living with, or my brother would pick Aidan up on a Friday and look after him until I got home. On

> Sunday, they'd look after him when I went to work in the morning, and drop him off while I was still at work.

Evan often says he was extremely lucky to be matched up with Karen. Not everyone is that lucky on their first attempt at internet dating. You could say—and Evan does—that it's almost like magic.

And now that you understand where Evan is coming from, let's get back to how our relationship works.

Chapter 7

Make Each Other Laugh

Our marriage started with laughter. Lots of it.

Our wedding was fun. Unlike many wedding days, ours was laid back and focused on fun.

And a lot less expensive.

> **EVAN:** My first wedding cost over $30,000. It was the whole package. We had a limo from 6 a.m. on the wedding day until we got to our hotel room at the end of the night. The photographer and videographer were also there for the whole day. We also both had huge families, so the venue and the catering cost a lot.
>
> When Karen and I got married, it was nothing like that. A few months before the big day, I heard an advertisement on the local radio station for a wedding show. There was a prize draw, with a top prize of $2,500 of wedding

services from some of the exhibitors at the show.

Karen bought her ticket online in advance, and from that moment on she felt that she was going to win the top prize.

On the day of the show, we were given our draw ticket when we checked in, and as we put our ticket into the box, Karen said to me, "We're going to win that top prize."

The draw came at the end of the event. They called the third prize winner, and it wasn't us. Then the second prize winner, and again it wasn't us. Then the announcer said, "and the winner of the grand prize, $2,500 to be spent with any of our exhibitors is…."

When they called out "Karen Gordon," she screamed and almost took off into the air with excitement.

The night before the wedding, we were up until 3 a.m. getting things ready. We did everything from creating our own centerpieces to hulling the strawberries and cutting the cheese. (No, not what you're thinking!)

Of course, weddings are a big production, even the second time around, so not everything went smoothly.

We had booked a room at a local hall for our reception. We had to get everything down there by 2 p.m. on the day before the wedding, so we were rushing around all morning, and when we got to the hall, we were horrified. The room wasn't set up! We had assumed that they would set out the tables and chairs for us, but that wasn't part of the deal. So with only a few hours to go, we were there hauling tables out of the storeroom and putting them up.

Luckily, we had used part of our prize money to hire a company to decorate the room for us. When they arrived, they joined in and helped us set up.

The company did such a good job of decorating the hall that the manager couldn't believe it was the same room and asked if he could take pictures. The hall has used those photos ever since, and they now hold weddings there regularly, so you could say we were trendsetters.

> **KAREN:** Some of Evan's relatives got the time mixed up, so the ceremony ended up starting thirty minutes late, but even that worked out well: having an extra half-hour to

sit around and wait really helped calm my nerves.

The ring bearer was Evan's great-nephew, who was only two years old at the time. Thankfully we had put fake rings on the pillow, because as he came down the aisle, he was swinging it around and dropping it. And every few steps he would try to give the rings to people. It was cute and funny all at the same time.

Why Laughter Matters

Laughter is important in a relationship, especially when times are difficult. Humor is a great way to make a point without coming across as threatening or overbearing, and it also helps to defuse tension and stress.

KAREN: I'm better now, but at one time I was always stressed out. I like to laugh every day because it really helps with the stress and makes life more enjoyable. Evan noticed that, and decided he would make me laugh every day. And he does: he even ended up writing it into his wedding vows.

Evan's Wedding Vows To Karen

I, Evan, stand here beside you, Karen, in the presence of God, family, and friends. I ask for your hand in marriage to become your husband, partner, friend and role model to your son Ryan.

I give to you my love, my heart and my promise of a lifelong membership of laughter, smiles and joy as long as I live and breathe. I will be with you in happiness and in sorrow. I will be there to keep you safe from harm and be your pillar of strength in times of need.

I have been blessed as, through your eyes, I can see you truly care for my son Aidan, who will look to you and Ryan as his family from this day forward.

My dream has now come true. My promise to Aidan is now fulfilled as you become my wife and our boys become brothers.

Karen, our marriage is a wonderful gift. I promise to cherish and invest in our relationship, our love, and our family as we grow and live together as one.

The biggest thing you can learn to do is to laugh at yourself. If you can laugh at yourself, then you can laugh at anything life throws at you.

We have both been in relationships where there wasn't the level of humor that we share now, and those were difficult relationships.

Life without humor is more combative. It becomes two people stating their point of view and battling to be right.

> **EVAN:** 90% of life is attitude, the other 10% is how you react to that 90%. I consider myself a very positive person. I surround myself with positive people, and she brings that out in me.
>
> Laughter, I learned a long time ago, is a powerful tool and I channel that into everything: my marriage, my parenting, even my work as a supervisor.
>
> **KAREN:** Evan drove Ryan to high school once, and as he dropped him off, Evan called out very loudly, "I love you, son!" Ryan just walked straight ahead as fast as he could, without looking back. We all have a good laugh thinking about it now!

Laughter is part of the intimacy that a couple shares. Ultimately, you can't take life too seriously, and there's a point where you have to be able to laugh at each other and with each other. Laughter brings you closer, and it can become self-sustaining: the more one partner laughs, the more the other laughs with them.

Of course, when a relationship is struggling, it can be hard to find much to laugh about, but something as simple as coming up with a fond pet name for your partner—not a cruel one—can be a start.

For example, our pet names for each other are Pookie and Sir Fartalot—we probably don't need to tell you who's who!

There is an instinct and an intuition to it: over time, you learn what makes your partner laugh. And equally importantly, what doesn't.

> **EVAN:** It's like a standup comedian. Sometimes he'll get heckled by the crowd, and he has to improvise. It's the same thing. It depends on what I'm faced with, I'll just use my life experience to make something funny or to get a chuckle out of her. Or I'll do something physical, like lifting my shirt up, to get her attention—especially when she's trying to focus on something—just to make her laugh and smile.
>
> Sometimes, of course, she's working, and she might be on a conference call. I know I can't interrupt her, so I'll pretend I'm walking in

slow motion, really quietly. She'll smile, and I know that I've caught her attention.

KAREN: On our first date, I don't remember a lot of laughs, but he talked a lot, and the conversation was interesting. Over the years, he has grown to know how important laughter is to me, too, so he's made an effort to get to know what makes me laugh and he puts the effort in to do it every day.

Sometimes Evan will put on a sad face and tell me that I have hurt his "feeling," and then I jokingly reply, "Oh well, it's only one of them, so it can't be all that bad."

Squirrels!

KAREN: Evan has the "squirrel" syndrome sometimes. He says he can't help himself and that he is attracted to shiny things: LED lights, tools, a good deal…you name it!

Back when we were planning our wedding, I took him to a store to get his opinion on some items I was thinking of for the big day. After a few minutes, I turned around and realized he was… missing! I had no idea where he had gone—as it turns out, the wedding section was close to the tool section, so off he trotted…

A staff member noticed me wandering around the store looking for something, and said "You look like you are looking for something. What can I help you find?"

I said "my fiancé."

She thought that was funny and asked what he looked like, then she went on a mission to find him, and she did.

She walked up to him and said, "Are you Evan?"

He said he was and she said, "Your fiancé is looking for you!"

Nice Pajamas, Evan!

A couple of summers ago, Evan got a little bit of an obsession. He was tired of dandelions, and he was determined that we weren't going to have any on our lawn, so he bought a special dandelion-removing tool. He loved going out on the lawn and pulling up all the dandelions with it.

The problem is, you can't just get rid of the dandelions in your own lawn: the seeds spread, so you have to clear them from your neighbors' lawns too.

> **KAREN:** We know our neighbors well, so Evan said to them, "If I see some dandelions, do you mind if I come over and pull them?" and they said that was fine.
>
> One Saturday morning, a little later, I noticed that Evan was missing. I couldn't figure out where he was. His truck was in the laneway, his shoes were in the hall, but he was nowhere to be found.
>
> After an hour, I was starting to get worried when I happened to look out of the kitchen window, and there he was, on the neighbor's lawn, in his pajamas and slippers!
>
> He'd seen a dandelion and gone to get it, but then he saw another, and another, and another, and the time flew by.
>
> I knocked on the glass and signaled him to come back inside. As soon as he realized I was watching him, he started to 'stalk' the dandelions, like a cat. So, suddenly he was jumping all over the neighbor's lawn, pouncing on dandelions!

> The funniest thing was that he felt he had to go get the dandelions in his PJs. I guess he was worried they'd hide while he got dressed!

"I Hear Boobies!"

Speaking of pajamas…

> **KAREN:** There was another time when Evan had been put on shifts again, so we became ships that pass in the night once more.
>
> One morning I was trying to get ready for work in the dark. Evan had only been home from work for a short time, and I wanted to let him sleep. So, there I was, half-dressed in the pitch black, when he suddenly sat up in bed and said, "I hear boobies!"
>
> It became one of those funny little things that he still does to make me laugh.

Why Doesn't Everyone Think This Way?

Not everyone is a born comic, of course. Some people are very analytical. Some are very serious. That's fine, but laughter can defuse a lot of tension in uncomfortable situations.

For some people, it's simply that they haven't learned the value of humor yet. It may even be that they haven't been through enough turmoil and pain to learn the value of being able to laugh at your misfortunes—that's certainly a major part of how Evan learned the lesson.

As a child, Karen discovered that making people laugh could lighten the mood. She also discovered the wonderful feeling you get when you bring happiness into someone's life.

> **KAREN:** I would try different things. If somebody said something funny, I would try to remember how they said it and what they said, and I would use that later in a different situation with different people.
>
> I try to look for the good in people and in situations. When someone does something well, I bring it to their attention, if I have the chance.

Even simple things have surprising power, and once you find that, it ignites a different kind of passion and makes the relationship that much better.

Just as important (for some couples, especially) is knowing when to stop; when you're in danger of going too far. If your relationship has become combative, laughter can quickly start to feel like mockery. But also, sometimes, your partner may just be trying to concentrate on something important, and they actually don't need—and don't appreciate—the laughter. So be sensitive to facial expressions and body language. Listen to their responses. Yes, they want to spend time with you, but they also know that they need to get the task they are working on done, and then they can give you their attention.

Rating

On a scale of 1-10, how good are you and your partner at making each other laugh?

Question

What are some of the things that make your partner laugh?

Making this work

- Whether you were the person who created the humor or not, watch what makes your partner laugh and notice, also, how laughter changes their mood.

- Think back to the last time you saw your husband or wife smile: what was it about? Why were they smiling? Build on that. If you truly haven't had a laugh in a long time or haven't seen each other smile in a long time, just go back to a time when you were smiling and laughing: remember that and build on that.

- Look back at your own childhood. Children have a wonderful sense of what makes grown-ups laugh, so bring that sense back into who you are now.

- First, learn to laugh at yourself. If you can't, then you are not going to be able to laugh. You have to love yourself so that you can laugh at the mistakes you make and fully appreciate your accomplishments.

Chapter 8

Commit To Making Her Feel Special

Winter in Southern Ontario is not pleasant. Every home should be issued by the government with a snow shovel in November, and a teenager to operate it. Until that happens, however, we have to make our own (teenagers, that is, not snow shovels: thankfully, we can get those at the local store).

Shoveling the driveway and playing "find my car" is a daily chore for at least three months of the year, and not something people look forward to.

It's the same routine every morning. Get up, down a quick cup of coffee, wrap up in several layers, spend half an hour digging out the car so that you can start the engine, just so that you can drive to work.

Except for that morning. When Karen stepped outside, something was different. At first, she thought that maybe it hadn't snowed overnight, but a quick glance at the neighbors' cars told her that it had snowed. A lot.

But her car was clear. It had been meticulously brushed clean. And the driveway had been shoveled clear too: even the ice dam the plows left by the sidewalk had been broken up and moved out of the way.

KAREN: Evan was working the night shift, and most mornings he'd come home just before I left for work. That morning he'd come home and noticed my car was snowed in. Even though he must have been dog-tired, he got the snow shovel and the brush out and set to work.

I don't like the cold, and I get cold easily. I really don't enjoy starting each day chiseling ice off the car, so it was wonderful to wake up and

> find that I didn't have to spend all that time out in the freezing cold, shoveling.
>
> He kept that routine going up until the spring. It was probably one of the nicest things anyone has done for me, especially as I'm not a morning person!

Starting your day with a wonderful surprise uplifts your mood and can make whatever goes wrong that day seem a little less problematic. Showing your partner that you care in very visible ways also helps bring the two of you closer. Plus, when you're the one who is creating the surprise, there is a wonderful payoff in seeing your partner's reaction.

One thing that works for us is that we both have strengths that balance the other's weakness. For example, one of us is a night owl, and the other is an early bird. Rather than letting those kinds of differences become a source of frustration, as some couples do, we've learned to appreciate the differences and to help each other compensate.

One way you can easily show you care for your partner is that if you see they are struggling with something that would be easy for you, it makes sense to help them out. This is your partner in life, the person you love and care about: show them how much you care.

> **KAREN:** Evan is a morning person. The alarm goes off, and within seconds he's on his feet. Me? I can't do that. It takes me a while just to get moving. Evan knows that, so if we have an early morning commitment, he will make me a cup of coffee and bring it to me. Instead of getting frustrated and mad that I'm not jumping out of bed, he tries to help me.

Little things like that change the quality of the relationship in a big way. They help to draw you closer together, and make it easier to feel passion for each other: it is much easier to feel physical love for someone who has invested emotionally in the relationship.

Too many relationships fall into the trap where one partner expects the other to be all over them in bed, but they are doing nothing for their partner outside the bedroom, and the tension starts to mount between them. How can you expect someone to want to share your bed when you can't bear to be in the same room together?

Another danger is when a couple starts to keep score. Doing something nice for your partner isn't just about getting a reward. Both sides—the caregiving and the reward—have to be given freely and because each of you wants to give it, not because of a misguided sense of obligation.

You should be thinking "I'll do this because I love her. I do this to improve the quality of her life," not, "I'll do this because then I can go to the pub with my friends on Wednesday."

Of course, when your partner does something nice for you, it is important to show them that you appreciate it too and to let them know. Tell them what difference it has made. Having that verbal 'thank you' is important. It's too easy to think, "Well, it's about time you did something for me." Instead, walk over and give them a hug or a kiss, say "thank you" or whatever you can think of to show that you recognize the thought they have put into their action.

> **KAREN:** It's not all one-sided. Evan shovels my car out in the mornings, but in the evening if it's snowing outside and Evan is watching the hockey game, I'll get my gloves and coat on, and I'll be out there clearing his car for the morning.

Ultimately, it's about working as a team to make things work.

Why Doesn't Everyone Think This Way

OK, we're going to make ourselves unpopular here, but look: if you do these things then we're not talking about you. We're talking about the ones who don't, so please: don't be offended.

The thing is, a lot of men are spoiled. They take things for granted.

It's easy to take someone for granted. Through life experiences, however, we have both come to realize that just because someone is in our life today, that does not guarantee they will be there tomorrow. With that in mind, commit to showing the people in your life how much you care for them.

We tried to raise our boys to be self-sufficient because we don't want them to ever be in the situation where they rely on their wives to do everything for them. We tell them, "we want you to be able to cook, clean, do your laundry, and all of that."

We're still looking forward to when they go to the grocery store and buy their own groceries and see the bill. That'll be an eye-opener!

Of course, it's not that people decide one day that they are "entitled": it started many years ago, at home—and it doesn't matter whether they're a man or a woman.

Some parents think it's their duty to do everything for their children and shield them from having to do anything, possibly because they think they'll have enough of it to do when they grow up, but it's important to have life skills that you can bring into a relationship.

Rating

On a scale of 1-10, how good are you at doing jobs that would 'traditionally' be allocated to your partner?

Question

Decide on one thing that you could do to lighten your partner's load that will make them feel special. Set a date for when you're going to do it.

Making this work

- Help with the household chores: make a meal; do the grocery shopping or help your partner carry it in and put it away; do the laundry (just remember to ask whether there are any special instructions if it's your first time!).

- Wash your partner's car and put gas in it.

- Make your partner their favorite drink (tea, coffee, or something stronger) and bring it to them.

- If you see your partner rushing to get something done so they can get out of the door, ask if there is anything you can do to help.

Chapter 9

Simple Things Score Big Points

Christmas Day. It was the first time Evan met Karen's dad, and their first Christmas together. He'd met her mother, but her father had always been busy working.

Ryan and Aidan had been given Nerf guns for Christmas, and they were running around the house being children.

Then Karen's dad spotted two more Nerf guns—the boys' old guns—sitting on a side table. "Evan, grab a gun!"

The hunt was on. Evan and Karen's dad started chasing the boys around the house, and the hunters had become the hunted.

In all the excitement, Evan tripped and started to fall down the stairs. Karen's dad spun around and caught him: it was hard to believe that the two of them were complete strangers just a couple of hours earlier. Talk about hitting it off!

They all loved it. It was the first Christmas Aidan had a playmate on Christmas Day, and he still calls it "the best Christmas ever!"

Why do the small things matter?

Put quite simply, doing the small things in the marriage can lead to big rewards.

It's important that you don't keep score, and never take each other for granted. When you do something small—brushing the snow off your partner's car, or putting away the laundry—they feel special because you are investing your time in them, and you are showing that you are committed for the long haul.

If you have spare time, take the opportunity to spend time with your partner: it is about prioritizing each other over everyone else.

KAREN: I have been in relationships before where my partner always wanted to be on the go. I'm someone who prefers to stay at home and relax if I have some free time, so it inevitably caused some tension.

Evan is very social, but he is also content to stay home talking to me and watching one of our favorite shows.

The wiper blades do what?

We live in an area where, a few winters ago, we had ice storms. That can make even a short commute very dangerous.

KAREN: At the time, there was a chance I would have to start commuting a few hours a day, so Evan was very concerned for my safety. He came home one day with heated wiper blades that help to stop ice from building up on the wipers. I didn't even know that kind of thing existed!

EVAN: In an ice storm, ice starts to build up on the wipers, and then they don't clear the windshield properly. So, suddenly, you're on

> the highway with cars all around you, and you can't see where you're going!
>
> These wipers defrost themselves. I also put in a heated washer system for good measure that helps clean the windshield.
>
> **KAREN:** I was dreading having to drive home on the highway in an ice storm because it can be treacherous. It meant a lot to me that he was concerned and was willing to help me be prepared.
>
> **EVAN:** Yes, I was. If she had to commute, I was going to make sure she made it home safe: good snow tires and an auto-dimming mirror with a rear-view camera, so that bright lights wouldn't be in her eyes.

And heated seats too?

A lot of people here in Canada have heated car seats. You spend a lot of time in the car in winter, so it's nice to be comfortable.

Not so many people have heated seats indoors, especially not heated toilet seats.

We do.

> **KAREN:** This is an older house, and both the bathrooms have the toilet right next to a window. Both of the windows are drafty, so the toilet seats get very cold.
>
> **EVAN:** I got fed up of being woken up from a dead sleep by Karen screaming "I'm freezing my butt off in here!"

So, Evan researched heated toilet seats. There were seats from Japan that cost $1,400 or more and even washed your important places for you. In the end, he found one closer to home. It doesn't wash anything, but it didn't cost $1,400, and Evan gets to sleep!

It's simply a matter of looking for opportunities to keep investing in the relationship and to provide some comfort for each other.

> **EVAN:** Karen studied Reiki, and when she got her Level 1, she started looking for a used treatment table. That Christmas, I got her a table. I support her in all her endeavors, in any way I can. And she finds ways to make my life better.

It comes down to listening to each other. Listening for a passing comment by your partner that they wish they had something. Noticing that they've been browsing reviews of something.

It's the kind of thing many couples do at Christmas, or when a birthday is coming up; you just have to get used to doing it all the time, not just at the traditional 'gift giving' times.

In the grand scheme of things, they are all very small things, so why do they mean so much?

Because it shows that you care, and you are willing to invest time and energy into doing those little things that mean a lot to your partner, that make their life easier.

It can be as simple as a koozie from the dollar store (a small knitted sleeve that goes over a beer bottle and keeps your hand warm and the beer cold).

> **KAREN:** Evan had a spare, and even though it was a Montreal Canadiens one, I kept using it. As it wasn't my team, he asked why I was using it, and I said, "Because I don't like touching the bottle. It's too cold on my hand."
>
> The neighbors had fun teasing me every time I turned up wearing a Maple Leafs jersey and holding a Canadiens koozie. They asked me if I was a confused fan or just having an identity crisis—all in fun, of course. In the end, Evan got me my own Maple Leafs koozie so I'd look more "normal."

Without all these little touches, there is no doubt our relationship would not be as close as it is. These small gestures add up, and they increase intimacy. Literally!

That's something to bear in mind. Often, guys only think about 'doing something nice' for their partner either once they're in the bedroom or when they're trying to get her there. It doesn't work that way. Women's minds are wired differently. A woman needs to know that her man cares, that he loves her, that he is in this for the long haul.

So, these small gestures outside the bedroom will pay off later. They could get you chasing each other for some "grown up time."

Women like to feel appreciated. Women like to know that somebody cares—that their guy cares—about them.

They also want to know that the person is listening. You don't have to buy anything, just listen. Then, when you listen, take action on what you heard. Actions really do speak louder than words.

Why doesn't everyone think this way?

So why doesn't everyone think this way, given what we just identified as the payoff?

Ultimately, they don't realize, or understand, what can happen if they start doing this. If they have never done the things that Evan does, or never done it to the same extent, then they don't realize that if they do a little bit here and a little bit there, it is going to make a big difference in their partner's life.

Often that is because it seems like such a small thing that they are doing, so they don't think it will get noticed or make a difference.

They assume that it takes grand gestures. A diamond necklace. A cruise. A new car.

But even the small things have big payoffs.

Diamonds are nice, but small thoughtful gestures (that might even be free) every day can make your partner's life more comfortable and bring a smile to their face.

Buying jewelry takes 10 minutes, and you can get the store to wrap it. But if you are constantly showing that you listen and you care, you are constantly building up goodwill and good feelings.

Rating

On a scale of 1-10, how good are you at identifying the little things that your partner wants and acting on it?

Question

What are three things you could do in the next week to show your partner you care and that they are important to you?

Making this work

- Bring your partner breakfast in bed. It is something that takes more thought than effort but will mean a lot.

- Run her a bubble bath and bring her a glass of wine.

- Light some candles and play some music.

- Take a stroll down memory lane and reminisce: talk about the happy, fun times the two of you have had together.

- Stick love notes in various places (no, not like that!) where your partner will find them.

- Say something nice about your partner to your friends and family on social media.

- Celebrate your partner's successes—even the small ones—especially if they mean a lot to them.

JOIN THE FUN

Come and join the fun on our Facebook page–you'll find a quiz like the ones we used to get to know each other better, as well as more stories and ideas to help you keep each other happy.

www.facebook.com/howmyhusbandkeepsmehappy/

Chapter 10

'Tis The Season To Be Stressful!

"I ruined Christmas!"

It was Christmas morning, and the turkey smelled... gamey? Funky? Who knew. Either way, it didn't smell right!

Karen had just taken the turkey out of the fridge. It was the first time she'd bought a fresh turkey, not frozen, and she'd been horrified to find a pool of sticky goo on the shelf in the refrigerator. That was when she saw the small cut in the bag.

When she opened the bag, it was even worse. It smelt bad. Frozen turkeys didn't smell like that, even when you'd thawed them.

If only she'd checked the turkey the day before. Better yet, if only she'd bought a turkey that wasn't in a damaged bag.

Now, with her parents on their way, Evan and Aidan on their way too, and all the stores closed for the holidays, she was faced with serving all the fixings and no turkey for Christmas dinner.

At that moment, Evan arrived and found her on the verge of tears.

"I think I just ruined everyone's Christmas." She told him about the cut in the bag, the goo in the fridge and the smell.

Evan sniffed the turkey. "Don't worry," he reassured her, "it's supposed to smell like that. Fresh turkey always smells a little when you open the bag."

Christmas used to be a very stressful time, as it is for many wives. Often, they find themselves having to organize Christmas singlehandedly—the work starts straight after Thanksgiving: buying presents for everyone, sending cards, planning and preparing the dinner—usually while holding down a full-time job as well.

It's fortunate that Evan realized what was going on and took over part of the Christmas madness. Not all couples are that lucky. Some husbands are quite happy to just invite their whole family over, and maybe even a few friends for good measure, and expect their wife to be chief cook, server, and dishwasher while they sit in the family room with the guests drinking beer.

It helps that Evan was brought up knowing how to cook. That Christmas he didn't just bring comfort and reassurance about the turkey: he'd also come ready to make two dishes of his own.

It's all part of how we approach everything: as a team. When a problem arises, it's "our" problem, and we aim to solve it together and figure out a way forward.

If your partner is telling you about a problem they have, it's probably because they can't figure it out on their own, and they need some help quickly.

And if they ask you to help solve a problem, you should be flattered. It's not a sign of weakness, it's a sign of respect: they respect your judgment and your opinion enough to come and ask for it.

One of the most interesting discoveries we made about each other was when we were taking marriage preparation classes before the wedding. Part of the course involved taking a test that measures how you deal with stress.

> **EVAN:** As in so many areas of life together, it turned out that we were perfect complements for each other: the test results suggested that stressful events didn't affect me very much, but Karen felt them a lot more strongly. She's a lot better at dealing with stress now, but back then her score suggested otherwise.

Evan's philosophy around stress is simple: he doesn't allow it. Stress is easy to control, as long as you have someone in your life who is willing and able to take that stress off you. In our marriage, that is what we do for each other.

That's the constructive way to handle stress in the relationship. The destructive way is to think, "I'm not going home. My wife (or husband) is too stressed out and too hard to be around at the moment, so I'll just stay out." That may help *you* and make things easier for *you*, but it's not helping your partner and it's not helping the situation.

Instead, find a way to defuse the situation and take the stress off them. Show them that you have their back. If this is the person you love and care for, then seeing them stressed should break your heart. If it doesn't—if you find it aggravating when your partner comes to you for help or dares to show that they are stressed—you need to ask yourself what's really going on.

The gift that keeps on giving

One of the greatest skills Evan brings to our relationship is organizing. Every couple needs at least one person willing to take on organizing Christmas.

Evan plans ahead. He's a doer. He'll put money aside every month for Christmas. If someone mentions something during the year that could be a Christmas gift for them, he'll remember it. And if they don't have it by December then that's what they're getting.

People think he's really good at choosing gifts, but actually, it's just that he's really good at listening, remembering and following up.

Stress is toxic

Time and energy are precious: too precious to waste being stressed out.

> **KAREN:** I always used to get sick at Christmas: I would try to do too much, and I would get so worn down that I'd catch something. Raising a child, working full-time, gift shopping, cleaning and decorating the house, and cooking the dinner proved to be too much for me.
>
> After our first Christmas together, Evan realized what was happening and announced that he was going to help by taking on some of the responsibilities.
>
> So now, Evan comes up with gift ideas and buys most of the gifts. He also helps shop for and cook Christmas dinner, and he helps clean and decorate the house—inside and out!

Stress is one of the most harmful things to a marriage. Left unchecked, it can drive a wedge between two people. Which is a real problem because, as you may have noticed, modern life is stressful. Life is full of potential stressors: children, work, household, money. These can break down a relationship very quickly.

Another source of stress in some relationships is when one partner keeps bringing up mistakes the other has made. That is something neither of us does.

> **EVAN:** I can't even remember the last time I was wrong. Not because I don't make mistakes, but because she never throws them in my face. I'll admit when I'm wrong, and I learn from it, and Karen never mentions it again.

Many couples keep poking at each other: "you did this last year," "you always do that." From there it builds up into a fight over the most trivial things: "you didn't put the toilet paper on the holder the right way" or "you didn't put the toilet seat down" or whatever it may be. We don't do that, even though—or perhaps because—we've seen relationships where that was the norm.

In fact, *not* bringing up past mistakes is probably one of the best things you can do to reduce your partner's stress levels! If you say you have forgiven something, you have to forget about it as well, and that means never bringing it up. Otherwise, you haven't really let go.

Rating

On a scale of 1-10, how good are you at handling stress?

On a scale of 1-10, how good is your partner at handling stress?

Question

What are three things you could do in the next week to relieve your partner's stress?

Making this work

- Learn to recognize the signs. Life is going to be full of stresses, and if you care enough about your partner, you need to know them well enough to spot when they are stressed.

- If you see your partner is stressed, ask them, "How can I help?" or "What can I do to lessen your burden?"

- At moments of high tension, don't be afraid to do something to ease the tension straight away.

Laughter can be a great stress reliever, as long as it is true laughter, so do something funny and spontaneous that will make them laugh.

- Reassure them. Tell them that it's going to be OK and that you'll get through it together. Even if you don't have the solution, talk about the steps you can take to *find* the solution: sometimes, the stress can simply be because your partner doesn't have a plan for resolving their challenge, so show them that there is a plan, even if you don't know the answer yet.

- Don't belittle their stress: accept it, and do something about it. Always remember that just because something doesn't seem important to you, doesn't mean it isn't important to your partner. If they are stressing out over something you think is minor, don't tell them that it doesn't matter, because to them it *does* matter. Right now, they need help, reassurance, and guidance, and they are looking to you as their partner to provide it.

Chapter 11

So Many Ways To Communicate

Communication is critical in a relationship because it is what allows you both to understand what your partner is thinking and feeling.

That knowledge of each other is the lifeblood of a marriage. If you don't have that, you don't have a relationship: you have a roommate you barely know.

Aside from conversation, though, communication is something that can happen all the time and in many different ways.

Over the years, we have been very inventive in finding different ways of communicating, even when our paths weren't crossing, and making it fun.

> **KAREN:** When Evan first moved in, he was working an early shift, and he'd be up and out of the door before the rest of the house was

> even awake. Each day, he'd find his lunch ready for him to take, and inside it was a love note.
>
> I had bought a block of pre-printed notes from a bookstore, and every night, I'd tear off the next note, add something of my own, and put it in his lunch box for the following day.
>
> It was just a quick, silly way of saying "I care, and I'm thinking of you," but Evan told me he really looked forward to reading the notes each lunchtime.

Simple things like that can mean a lot. A note, an email, a call or even a text, when they're unexpected, can transform your partner's day. Especially if their day hasn't been going well.

Do you have good communication?

People start yelling when they feel they are not being heard. If you have good communication, you don't yell at each other. You might yell at other people if you're mad—and sometimes you may even yell at them together—but you don't yell at each other.

So, apart from an absence of yelling, how do you know if the communication you and your partner have is good?

First, watch their responses. Watch their body language. Look for a smile. Track their mood.

> **EVAN:** Sometimes, if Karen is talking to me and she doesn't feel she has my full attention, she'll flash her boobies at me (only in the privacy of our own home, of course!). After that, she definitely has my full and undivided attention!

Second, get to know your partner's 'normal' level of energy: both physical energy, and verbal energy. For example, Evan has very high verbal energy. If he's talking, then he's happy and engaged. If he goes quiet, then you know something's wrong.

If your partner is normally very low energy in their communication, however, then silence from them isn't necessarily a bad thing. That's their *normal*.

> **EVAN:** In early 2016, I suffered two concussions. The first time, I slipped on ice in a parking lot and fell backward. I didn't have a chance to brace myself, and my head smacked the concrete. A little while later I started to have problems: I had a high pitched ringing in my ears, and I couldn't stand bright lights.
>
> Just a month earlier, one of my uncles had died from a fall after hitting his head, so when I told

> Karen what had happened, she said she would take me to Emergency.
>
> **KAREN:** As we sat waiting to be admitted, Evan wasn't himself. He was very quiet, and when he did speak, it didn't make sense.
>
> **EVAN:** Ten days later, I got hit on the back of the head—in exactly the same spot!—by a fire extinguisher that rolled off a shelf.
>
> **KAREN:** For months after that, he wasn't himself. The ringing was back, and the trouble with bright lights. He started to forget things—which definitely isn't like him—and he had lost his wonderful sense of humor.

One of the long-term effects the doctors warned us about was the possibility that his personality would change. That was a worry for both of us: we liked Evan just the way he was!

When a partner changes like that, you know something is wrong. In this case, we knew the problem was a medical one and had a cause. For most couples, though, it may just be that your partner has something going on, and maybe they need to communicate about it but can't find the right way.

Make time to communicate

As we've said, there are many ways to communicate, and it's good to explore different avenues.

Circumstances forced those different approaches on us: Evan's shift work meant that we didn't have much time together, and we had to find other ways to connect. But shift work isn't the only thing that can stop a couple communicating, so the same approach and techniques that helped us connect when time was a problem—quizzes, notes, etc.—can also help when there are other barriers.

Our favorite way to communicate, though, is face-to-face. Evan is a chatterbox; he loves to talk. Not all men are like that, but everyone should make time to sit down and talk.

The adaptation works both ways. We both work full-time, and sometimes it's one of us working odd hours and weekends, sometimes it's the other.

> **KAREN:** I currently work from home, which has taken some adjustment for both Evan and I. Before, when I had an office job, being home meant Karen-Evan time. Now, I sometimes work in the evenings, so even though I'm in the house, Evan can't have my undivided attention.

> Evan understands, and he knows that I am thrilled to be working in the personal development industry. Plus, there are perks to my job: I recently got to meet Bob Proctor in person!

When the day is done, let it be done. Put the smartphone away, turn off the laptop, grab a glass of wine or whatever, and make time to sit together and talk.

It can be tempting for men to fall back on the stereotype of being the 'strong, silent' type, and under-communicate. Hopefully, this book is making you appreciate that communication is important to the woman in your life.

So, if it is important to your wife, bite the bullet and make it important to you. It doesn't have to be all the time, but just once in a while. You don't have to do everything she wants to do; just make sure that sometimes you remember to do something she wants to do.

Rating

On a scale of 1-10, how good are you and you partner at communicating with each other?

Question

What are three things you could do in the next week to communicate your love to your partner?

Making this work

- Sit in the dark with your partner and have a conversation. This will ensure that you are not distracted by other things and your focus in on your partner and their voice.

- One person starts a sentence, and their partner finishes it. Then switch.

- Each pick one topic to discuss. Perhaps it is a challenge or problem you have that you would like your partner's input on.

- Each say a couple of words that explain why you love your partner, for example, "I feel safe and supported when you're around."

- Come up with a pet name for your partner and explain why you picked that name.

- Write a short letter or make a short video explaining why you love your partner.

Chapter 12

She's Number One

Evan's work shifts have been a big influence on how we manage our relationship. That doesn't mean that if neither you nor your partner works shifts then what we have learned has nothing to do with you. Many relationships have something that could "get in the way." What our marriage has taught us is that if you want to make a relationship work, you adapt and adjust; you work around the obstacles.

At one point, for about two and a half years, Evan was on yet another weird shift. And yet again, it was playing havoc with married life. Sunday through Thursday, he would work the night shift. Friday morning he would come home, sleep, and then spend the afternoon getting a nice dinner ready. Friday night would be date night, and we'd be together Saturday and Sunday. The rest of the week, when one of us was coming home, the other would be leaving for work, and we didn't see each other.

A few years ago, the company Evan was working for organized a dinner cruise for the staff. It was on a Saturday night: one of only two nights a week that we got to spend together. To make matters worse, it was seen as a team-building exercise, so it was staff-only: partners weren't invited!

Some husbands might have gone anyway, but Evan refused. His boss threatened to make it mandatory, so Evan threatened to resign!

So, while Evan's work colleagues went off on a boat to talk about work, we stayed home, fired up the grill, and watched the sunset on our deck.

That was how he wanted to spend his Saturday night.

> **KAREN:** I didn't have a problem with him going on the cruise. I told him to go—especially if it meant losing his job—but he insisted.
>
> I was flattered that our time together was that important to him.

Now, you might be thinking that's an odd choice of words: "flattered." It sounds like something you'd say when you're first seeing someone, not when you've been together for 10 years. But that's the thing: one of the reasons our relationship is as close as it is, is that we work to keep it feeling fresh and new, as though we were still dating. We focus on keeping the flame alive.

Karen has Silly Ass Disease

Karen can look back at this story and laugh now, but she didn't find it funny at the time…

> *"Karen has Silly Ass Disease, so there's a lot of stuff she can't eat."*
>
> *Evan's brother looked at him with a puzzled expression. "Are you* sure *that's what it's called?"*
>
> *"Yep." Evan was firm. "That's what she told me. She has Silly Ass Disease. She can't eat bread."*
>
> *Later, when Karen found out what Evan had said, she was horrified. "It's celiac disease! CE-LI-AC! Gluten intolerance!"*
>
> *Of course, it's been "Silly Ass Disease" in our family ever since!*

Something as simple as a food intolerance or an allergy can put a surprising strain on a relationship. Anything that restricts what one partner can do could be a problem if the other partner is forced to make sacrifices to accommodate it.

Celiac disease came up on our second date. We were sitting at the restaurant table, and the server brought a basket of bread for the table.

> **KAREN:** I thought it could be an issue for some people, so I wanted to bring it up early. Sharing meals is important in a relationship, so I wanted it out in the open. When Evan offered me a roll, I just said "It's bread. I can't eat it." Then I explained I had celiac disease. Evan had never heard of it, so to try and remember the name, he thought of it as "silly ass disease." And that's what he mistakenly told his family. And the neighbors. And the people at work. And all his friends!
>
> I found out when we got invited to dinner by his brother and sister-in-law. I was worried about the food, and Evan tried to reassure me. "Don't worry," he said. "I know you don't like to talk about it, so I told everyone you have silly ass disease. I told my whole family, so you don't have to explain it."

I thought he was joking, so I was waiting for him to break into laughter. When I realized he was serious, I was horrified. I reminded him of the correct name, and I could see the lightbulb go on in his head.

I remember walking into my future in-laws' house for the first time, shaking Nancy's hand and saying, "Hi, nice to meet you, I don't have silly ass disease. It's called celiac disease, and it's not contagious!"

EVAN: In the early days, I'd forget. For example, Karen loves pumpkin pie, and there's a place near where I used to live called The Apple Factory; they make the most amazing pies. So one day on the way home from work I stopped by and bought her a pumpkin pie. I was so pleased with myself, and Karen was appreciative, but she didn't seem very keen to eat it. Then she started scraping the topping off into a bowl so she could eat it! That was when I remembered that the crust had wheat in it.

After that, I started reading all the labels.

He has also adjusted his cooking. It's simply another way of showing his love, his respect and how much he cares.

EVAN: I also found that I prefer rice pasta over wheat pasta: it has a better taste and texture. It's harder to cook, though, because you can overcook it very easily and it turns to mush, so there was some trial and error involved. I learned how to make white sauces with cornflour instead of flour.

I am always on the lookout for new gluten-free foods to try.

Pizza was something that was huge for us. Date night on a Friday usually meant that I'd get a pizza delivered, but Karen had to have frozen pizza from the gluten free aisle at the supermarket. They're not great: a bit like a slab of drywall with some tomato sauce poured over it. She tried to jazz them up with her own toppings, but it still wasn't the same. She'd say "Do you know how lucky you are to eat pizza? I'd love to have a pizza from a pizzeria."

One day I was passing a pizza place, and they had a sign that read "Gluten-Free Pizza Sold Here!" Finally, she could have pizza that wasn't frozen, and we could get it delivered.

Clamming up

As a family, we love seafood. Fish, shellfish: it's all good. Aidan loves it. Ryan loves it. The only family member who doesn't like seafood is Evan. He won't let it past his lips, which is ironic because he makes a great seafood chowder. And yet, he has no idea just how good it is: when he makes it, he even has to get Karen, Ryan or Aidan to taste it and check the seasoning.

> **EVAN:** Campbell's used to make gluten free chowder, and Karen loved it, but we can't find it anymore. I knew how to make corn chowder and potato chowder, so I did some research. I got scallops, crabmeat, and clams and I made it all up in a pot.
>
> It was Christmas Eve, and Garth and Nancy—Karen's dad and his partner—were coming over. I knew how much Karen and the kids enjoyed it, so I wanted to make it for them too!

Since then, the chowder has become a family Christmas tradition.

So corny…

You'll have noticed that food features in a lot of our stories. It featured in our relationship from the earliest days.

An early experiment was cornbread. You'd think cornbread would be gluten free anyway, but it isn't. Most commercial cornbread has wheat flour in it.

One of our early dates was at Montana's Barbecue and Bar, one of a chain of restaurants here in Canada. One of their specialties is cornbread, and it is *sooo* good!

Evan was determined that silly ass disease shouldn't get in the way of Karen enjoying any food she liked, so he decided he was going to make cornbread.

> **KAREN:** The first attempt was with a commercial kit for gluten free cornbread. Everything came in a bag, and you just had to mix it with eggs and water. It was awful. I'd tried a bite of the cornbread at Montana's, and this was nothing like it!
>
> Evan spent an hour or so researching recipes online. He couldn't find one recipe that sounded right, so he ended up combining a dozen different recipes that included things like brown sugar, molasses, and buttermilk.

> **EVAN:** Each recipe gave different instructions for how to mix the ingredients, and in what order, so there was a lot of trial and error. The first attempt came out like a rock, the second was doughy, and on the third, it came out just right, but I hadn't made a note of what I was doing! It took me another six tries before I got it right again. It ended up costing $80 to figure it out, but now I have the recipe written down, and I make it regularly for Karen.

The key thing is that Evan's attitude isn't, "Well, you were born with this, so tough luck: you have to miss out." Instead, he tries to accommodate gluten free. He approaches it like a puzzle to be solved: "How can I make sure Karen doesn't miss out on anything just because of her dietary needs?"

Why this matters

It's all about how a couple deals with challenges.

One approach would be for the partner who doesn't have a problem to say, "Too bad. You can't keep up with me." There are partners who will do that and will treat it as a flaw or weakness.

The alternative is to realize that your partner has a challenge and to do everything you can to help them live with it. If you love someone and you are committed to them, that's the only approach that makes sense.

A lot of people might think that all of these things we do are over the top.

We don't see it that way at all.

Think of your marriage like a cup.

If you let the cup get drained, you have to fill it up again, and that takes time and effort. It's much easier to keep the cup topped up all the time: you take a sip, you add a sip back.

Everything we do has a simple purpose: to make our life together better.

We each want the other to know that our relationship is foremost in our daily life and routine; that they are the person we look forward to coming home to and being with after a day at work.

> **EVAN:** I put my heart and soul into making Karen feel there is a man in her life that wants to be a part of her world and to make her world never stop spinning. I get even more motivated when I see her smile or laugh, or she embraces

me with a warm hug. To know that I have someone in my life who makes me feel that I'm number one in her world is my greatest reward.

Put down the fork

Evan loves to cook—you've probably noticed that by now—but he doesn't like to do the dishes, and we don't have a dishwasher.

The first time he cooked a meal in what is now "our" kitchen, he would put down a fork, and when he went to pick it up, it had disappeared.

> **KAREN:** "I wasn't used to having nothing to do in the kitchen; that just doesn't happen as a single mother. So every time he put something down, I'd wash it. He'd say "didn't I just have a spoon there? Can I have it back, please?"
>
> I thought, "What am I doing? Why don't I just go do something else or take a break?" It took a little while to get used to the idea that there was someone else to help; someone else in the partnership. But I certainly welcomed the idea!

Sometimes, the most meaningful gestures are the ones you least expect. Like cheering the other side.

Evan is a big fan of the Montreal Canadiens hockey team. While we were writing this book, they were having the best start to their season ever, and their goalie got his 10th straight win on home ice—something that has never been done before. It was a big night.

> **EVAN:** Karen was tired, to the point where she could barely keep her eyes open. But she stayed up to watch it with me. She knew how much it meant to me.

Evan said, "It's history in the making." That was the song we had our first dance to at our wedding, so it would have been hard to go at that point.

> **EVAN:** That small act meant a lot to me. Especially as Karen is a Toronto Maple Leafs fan!

Sometimes, you do something because it feels natural, so you may not even know you are doing it, but it means a lot more than you realize to your partner.

Now, let's sound a note of caution here. What we're talking about is not putting your partner on a pedestal. It's not about always putting your own needs and wants second to theirs. Neither of us does that, and neither of us would ask anyone else to do that.

What we are talking about is simply looking for opportunities to show that your relationship is your priority.

When you put someone on a pedestal, it's hard work.

Earlier, we said that a relationship is like a car: you keep it serviced, you change the oil, you fill the tank, you make sure the washer fluid is topped up. It's about keeping the car in top condition so that it will run well. If you really care about the car, you buy a good brand of oil, and you might put a higher rated gas in the tank. You spend a little more on tires. In other words, you invest.

Then there's the people who get a little obsessive about their car. They polish it by hand every day, inside and out—even the tires. It stays under a dustsheet, inside a garage with a better air conditioning unit than the house. And the car only gets taken out twice a year, on days when the weather forecast is absolutely perfect.

That's high maintenance!

> **EVAN:** Putting my wife first is not a bad thing. I look at it this way: she is my soul mate. I can read her like this book. I know what's important to her, what she is feeling and thinking. I also know that I'm #1 in her life,

> which is an even trade. Giving my wife my time, my attention and even my advice, if asked for, only strengthens our relationship. My instinct is to listen to her eyes and see with my ears. That may sound crazy, but it works. I listen to her body language and see the words she is telling me. To be that in tune with someone is magic. We often find ourselves finishing each other's sentences or bringing up a topic that the other was just thinking about. It's like having a sixth sense that compliments my marriage and draws us even closer.

Many wives worry that they already have responsibilities to the kids, then the cat or dog, the house, their job: there's barely any energy left for themselves as it is, so if they have to put their husband first as well, then there will be nothing for them.

That's not the case.

Remember. You are a team. You are both dealing with all of that. By giving your partner that love and attention, they will be there to give you the support and boost you need when you need it. You won't have to ask for help; it will be there.

And that works both ways. By putting each other first, without waiting for your partner to do it first, you create a virtuous circle: you get out what you put in.

> **EVAN:** That is how my grandparents were. Family was everything to my grandfather: it was his foundation, his wellbeing. My grandmother was his soul mate, and without her, he was lost. They did chores together in the morning in the barn. He would be out in the field working, and she was there bringing him lunch. If he was out cutting wood for the stove and the furnace, she was there right beside him. They were inseparable. When they weren't together, they were awkward. They didn't hold hands, and there wasn't a lot of hugging and kissing, but I could see their love. When my grandfather passed away, my grandmother followed soon after. I am sure it was due to a broken heart, because she was totally lost without him.

But I work all day...

Many couples today are in the situation where both partners work, whether full-time or part-time, but that's not the case for all couples. It's one thing to say "put your partner first," but what happens when one partner is working full-time and the other isn't?

It's tempting for the working partner to say, "Look, I do put you first: I go out to work all the time so you can stay home." That isn't going to sit well with the partner who is staying home, bringing up the children. In fact, it can feel like they're saying the exact opposite: "You're not as important as me because I'm the one earning all the money."

Remember that your partner is the one making it possible for you to come home to a house that is livable. They could equally say, "I'm doing everything here so that you can come home from work and not have to start cleaning and cooking."

For the stay-at-home partner, it can be a lonely life. While one of you is out at work, and probably gets to talk to other people and interact, they are at home talking to the washing machine and the dog.

> *A man comes home one evening from work, and finds the kids out in their pajamas playing in a puddle and the dog running around loose. He panics and flies indoors, wondering what has happened to his wife. Inside, he finds the kitchen in darkness and no dinner ready. There is dog food all over the kitchen floor, and dirty dishes piled up.*

He runs upstairs, convinced something terrible must have happened, but when he bursts into the bedroom, he finds his wife on the bed with a glass of wine, watching TV and eating chocolate.

"What's going on? You had me worried!" he says.

She replies, "You know when you come home every day, and you say, 'What did you do all day?' Well, today I didn't do it."

Author unknown

Rating

On a scale of 1-10, how good are you at showing your partner that they are your priority?

Question

What are three things you could do in the next week to show your partner they are a priority in your life and important to you?

Making this work

Showing your partner that they are your priority doesn't have to mean spending a lot of money.

- Is there a show your partner really enjoys, but can't watch because of their commitments? Record it for them and then watch it together on date night. The great thing about this is that it will earn you brownie points whether you like the show yourself or you don't. If it's a show you hate, your partner will appreciate that you are watching it with them; if it's one that you love, your partner will appreciate that you waited to watch it together!

- If dinner out at a restaurant is outside the budget, put together a picnic or set up date night at home. Put thought into it and put effort into the treats.

- On your way home from work, call your partner and ask if there is anything they need. Better yet, surprise them with something you know they need or would like.

- If you know there is something your partner is going to ask you to do, do it without waiting to be asked. The trash gets picked up on the same day every week: take it out without waiting to see if they'll take it out instead.

- Put time and effort into things that will please your partner. Wash their car, make them breakfast: the opportunities are there if you look for them.

- Tackle something on the "Honey Do" list.

- Instead of saying things like "you always/never do this…", say "I know you are busy, but if you could help me with X, I'd really appreciate it."

Chapter 13

Respect, Trust, and Loyalty

Respect, trust, and loyalty are the foundation that a relationship is built on, and you need a strong foundation if you want the relationship to grow and flourish. You can build your relationship on sand, or you can build it on rock.

Our relationship is built on mutual trust, mutual respect, and mutual loyalty. We value each other's opinion, and we ask for it.

Having your partner's respect validates that you are on the right track. If you value your partner and your relationship, then you put effort into it, and that includes respecting your partner's wishes, views, and opinions. That doesn't mean that you always have to let them have their way. It means that you act as a team, and you make decisions together.

"I want a motorcycle"

Remember that big payoff we mentioned earlier in the book?

Evan has been talking about getting a motorcycle since 2014. His brother has a bike, his three cousins have bikes, our neighbor has a bike. In fact, Evan was the only one without a bike.

He finally got one in spring 2016: a Suzuki GW250F. It's not a big, fast bike, but it is economical to run and easy to maintain.

> **EVAN:** When I asked Karen if she was OK with me buying a motorcycle, her immediate concern was for my safety. It wasn't the money—and remember that as well as the cost of the bike, you have to factor in a few thousand dollars for safety gear and clothing.
>
> "Riding a bike can be dangerous, Evan," she said, and I replied, "That's not what I asked."
>
> We discussed why I wanted one, and the fact that I had owned a bike when I was in my 20s. She could see how much it meant to me, and finally, she asked how I was going to pay for it.
>
> "I'll look after that," I said. "I just want your blessing to have a motorcycle."

> She was good with that and said, "If you really want one, have it." She also added that I'd never get her to ride it, though! Even so, I keep asking. Maybe one day she'll go for a ride.
>
> **KAREN:** He'd been driving around in an old '93 Ford truck with over 200,000 miles on the clock for six years so that we wouldn't have any monthly payments: it was his way of saving money for the family. So, I thought he deserved to have what he actually wanted.

For Evan, asking was natural. Not because of the money or because of the risk, but because we make big decisions together. We are a team, and we respect and value each other's opinion.

If you don't have an open and honest relationship, you have nothing. If you can't tell each other when something is bothering you, you have nothing. It's important to have trust and honesty as the foundation of your relationship, then build on that foundation one brick at a time.

Listen to each other's wishes, dreams, and aspirations, then work together and support each other in getting them.

When you have that kind of relationship, you don't need to keep secrets from each other.

Respect is also about recognizing that you each have strengths and weaknesses. Men and women are wired differently. Something that annoys you may not even register with your partner, and vice versa. Rather than using your differences as a source of conflict, enjoy the fact that you complement each other, and draw on each other's strengths to build a team that, together, can achieve anything!

Trust and loyalty

Respect and trust are tied together. They cannot be separated. When you respect someone, you also trust them: if you couldn't trust them, then how could you respect them?

In a relationship, trusting your partner means knowing that the way they act when you are around is also the way they will act when you are not around.

Loyalty is more than being faithful. It is a daily choice, to always be there for your partner; to always be someone they can count on. Especially when they aren't asking for it: when you have a close relationship, you can sense when your partner needs your help, even if they don't say that they do.

Loyalty can be as simple as holding your time together sacred, and not letting anything get in the way of that (for example team building dinner cruises!)

When one of us is out and sees something we think the other would like, we'll buy it. Not because we were asked to, but because we know it will bring our partner pleasure. It might be sushi (even though Evan hates fish), a chocolate bar, or a bottle of Evan's favorite beer: there are lots of little things that can bring a smile to your partner's face.

> **EVAN:** I knew a couple who aren't together anymore. The wife was on the heavier side, and you could hear her coming down the stairs. The husband would say things like: "your steps are getting louder. Are you putting on weight?" That's not a recipe for a happy marriage—even as a joke. It's no surprise they went their separate ways.

People change over time—physically as well as mentally. Even if you weighed 115 pounds when you met your partner, as you get older your metabolism changes; it slows down. You have kids. Things start to sag.

Men change too. They lose their hair. They get pot bellies.

None of that matters if you truly love each other.

You have to love the person from inside out. Physical appearance is important, but you have to be in love with the inner person as well.

Of course, respect, trust, and loyalty do not come automatically: they have to be earned. That starts with how you behave towards your partner: honoring their wishes, defending them when someone attacks them, following through on your promises, not lying or keeping secrets.

Honey, you're wrong...

As a couple, you should never try to catch your partner out and tell them they are wrong—we've seen many couples do that over the years (and pay the price).

Sometimes, though, you do need to tell your partner they are making a mistake, especially if it is going to get them in trouble or make them look bad to the outside world. In fact, in those circumstances, it is your job as a loving partner to protect them.

Knowing when to pick your battles is a big part of earning your partner's respect. If they know that you only say 'no' when it's for their own good, then they will respect your opinion and ask for it.

So the question then is how do you tell the person you love that they are wrong in a loving and caring way?

It's down to how you say it. You can't lead in with "What were you thinking?" or telling them they're wrong outright. Open the conversation with something that puts your comments in context: "Honey, I love you, and I'm only telling you this because I'm trying to protect you and care about you, so don't do that."

Then add more detail: "I feel X is going to happen." Or "I feel that you are going to be harmed if you do that."

If you've been burned before

We are both ordinary people, both on our second marriage, and both with very little reason to trust when we came into this relationship. You, too, may have negative experiences in your past that make it harder to trust.

The first thing you have to learn is not to dwell on those past experiences, and certainly never to compare your current partner to your ex—even if they come out on top in the comparison!

Of course, it may also be that you have had your trust violated in your current relationship, and you are trying to come back from that as a couple.

Either way, you may find that you have unrealistic expectations. Often, when someone has been hurt in the past, they become controlling. They want to know where their partner is going, what they are doing, who they are with. They check up on them and try to catch them out. They demand that their partner agrees with them 100% on everything. So instead of a relaxed relationship, it becomes tense and confrontational.

It's like taking a dog for a walk on a short lead: the dog will pull against it and try to go its own way, and the owner pulls against the dog and tries to force them to go their way. In the end, neither of them enjoys the walk, they're both exhausted, and neither of them looks forward to the next time!

Now you might be thinking, "but why would someone stay in a relationship like that?" There are many couples who do. They might stay together for the children, or because their culture doesn't allow them to separate, or simply to please their parents.

Or they might stay because they remember what it was that attracted them to their partner in the past, and they know that it could work again.

If you are going to stay, then make a go of it. Start by giving your partner a chance to prove that they can be trusted. That means that you have to let them be free and make their own choices, because—as we said earlier—loyalty is a choice, and in order to choose loyalty, there has to be the opportunity (not taken) to be disloyal. You have to give your partner some freedom and see what they do with that freedom. That can be scary—for both of you—but it is the only way your partner will be able to win (or win back) your trust.

You have to forgive and forget. That means you have to forgive your ex (if they were the one that hurt you) or your partner (if it was them). You also have to forget—which, as we said earlier, means that you don't keep dredging up the past every time your partner does something wrong.

You also have to forgive one more person and forget, and that is yourself: stop beating yourself up over your own past mistakes. If you don't forgive yourself, and you don't let go and forget, then you will forever be second-guessing yourself.

These are not easy things to do, but if you truly value the relationship and want it to work, then you have to do it.

Rating

On a scale of 1-10, how good are you at forgiving and forgetting?

On a scale of 1-10, how good is your partner at being loyal and supportive?

Question

What are three things you could do in the next week to show you are loyal to your partner and trust them?

Making this work

- Keep your commitments to your partner. Your word is your bond. If you said you would do something, then follow through with it.

- Respect boundaries and if your partner is sensitive about a certain topic then don't mention it.

- Compliment and support your partner in front of others.

Chapter 14

Engage In Conversation

Conversation is a big part of keeping a relationship happy and together. All too often these days, you'll see a couple sitting in a coffee shop, and they are both engrossed in their phones or tablets. They might as well be there alone.

Even when we are sitting in the family room in the evening with the TV on, we are chatting—unless Dateline is on, or the hockey game!

Sometimes, we'll go into town to a coffee shop or a restaurant, but we prefer quieter ones where we can talk.

We talk a lot about what's going on, and about our sons; we'll make plans for the weekend or, better yet, for the future.

The key to conversation, however, is engagement. You can tell from your partner's body language whether they are engaged: are they looking at you, or over your shoulder (or worse still out to the side)? Are they nodding and acknowledging what you say, or do they seem distant and distracted? Are they asking questions that match what you're saying, or just giving the occasional 'uh-huh'? And if you ask them a question, does the answer show that they were listening, or do they struggle to figure out what you expect them to say?

Why this matters

Conversation is part of intimacy. Intimacy starts long before you get in the bedroom. It starts in the morning of that day: if you aren't getting along and communicating that day, it's going to be difficult to end up being intimate that evening.

Humans—and especially women—need to interact to feel close. Women have to be emotionally and physically engaged in the conversation and need their partner to be engaged too.

A woman also wants to know that she is being heard. You need to feed back to her in a way that shows you heard what she said and took it on board.

> **EVAN:** Our marriage is not perfect by any means: we're evolving all the time. We both

> make mistakes, but we learn not to make the same mistake twice. It's like a child learning to walk: if they want to walk, they are going to fall over, but they get back up and continue to walk.

So, even though we have the same challenges as other couples, we make it work because we want to. We value this relationship, and we are both emotionally invested in it.

Blood from a stone: how to get your silent partner talking

If your partner is not the talkative type, getting them to engage in conversation can feel hard.

Start with topics that he is interested in (we're going to assume for this bit of the chapter that it's the husband who doesn't like to chat, but it could be the wife, in which case, just swap 'he' for 'she'). Show some interest yourself in those topics. Get him to explain the subject in general first, then get him to explain what he most enjoys about it or what makes it interesting for him.

After you've shown a genuine interest in his favorite topics, you can ease the conversation into the areas you want to talk about.

If you're really serious about making things work, the ultimate effort could be to take a course or start participating in one of your partner's key interests. That is the ultimate way to show warmth, love, and respect. You never know, you may discover a new shared passion!

> **KAREN:** I grew up in a house where the hockey game was always on in the background. When I realized what a big hockey fan Evan is, I decided to get more involved and watch the games with him.
>
> This turned into friendly ribbing whenever the Toronto Maple Leafs and the Montreal Canadiens are playing, and whoever's team wins gets to do their "Happy Dance" around the coffee table!

Get the conversation going

In the last section, we assumed the man doesn't want to talk, and the woman does. But what if you're the usually silent husband and you want to start the conversation going yourself?

A good way to start can be a sincere compliment. A key piece of advice here is to compliment her on her choices, not her genetics. In other words, comment on how nicely she has done her hair, or how much you like the clothes or a piece of jewelry she is wearing.

Commenting on some aspect of her anatomy is great, but it's flirting not conversation. That doesn't mean you shouldn't tell your partner how beautiful (or handsome) they are, but that's a different topic.

Another way to start the conversation is by doing something nice for her.

> **KAREN:** Evan will often start the weekend off by bringing me up a coffee while I'm still in bed, then we sit and drink our coffee together and chat.

Also, listen for the topics your partner likes to talk about. There are some subjects women like to talk about that men generally don't (emotions, the latest gossip, you know the kind of thing!), so surprise her and start the conversation with one of those.

Our first Valentine's Day together

On our first Valentine's Day, we made a fire and lit candles and settled town to watch a movie.

> **EVAN:** I told Karen she could pick any movie she liked. When she told me she wanted *Mamma Mia*, I swallowed hard. I'd been hoping she wouldn't choose a chick flick.
>
> **KAREN:** All through the movie, every time I looked across at Evan, he had a shocked look on his face. His eyes were as big as saucers, and his mouth was wide open!
>
> Later he confessed it was all an act, and he'd really enjoyed the movie.

What I learned from Bob Proctor

Bob Proctor teaches a great principle, which is to "leave people with the impression of increase." What that means is that you should aim to make people feel better for having interacted with you. When you do that, people enjoy being around you, and you become a more attractive personality.

The funny thing is, even when people are very good at living by that principle when they are dealing with strangers, they sometimes forget to be like that at home with their loved ones. Perhaps it comes down to a feeling that if two people are in love, then they should feel better around each other automatically. Whatever the reason, stop it! You should aim to make your partner feel better for being around you.

That means that you give them a chance to say what's on their mind, and you let them know that they are being listened to when they do. It means giving positive feedback. It can also mean noticing all the positive qualities your partner has.

Rating

On a scale of 1-10, how good are you at meeting your partner's emotional needs?

On a scale of 1-10, how good is your partner at reading your body language?

Question

What are three new (and interesting to them!) topics you could talk about with your partner?

Making this work

- Pay your partner a sincere compliment. Say something positive about them.

- Do something small for them that they will appreciate.

- Know when and when not to, solve the problem.

- Set the tone of your conversation by incorporating laughter. This can help ease tension and make conversations more enjoyable.

- Make an effort to listen when it is your turn to listen, and talk when it's time to talk.

- On date night, let your partner pick the movie and go with it—you never know, you might enjoy it!

Chapter 15

The Little Things Go A Long Way

Evan looked at the tears in Karen's eyes. "What is it? Did I do something wrong?" he asked, concerned.

"No," she answered. "You won't believe this, but I've never had ice cream in a cone!"

What brought on this show of emotion?

Just a simple ice cream cone, but with one special characteristic: it was gluten free. Evan had spotted it in the supermarket and bought a pack. It was a simple gesture, but to someone who has always had to watch in envy as other people enjoyed their ice cream cones, it meant the world.

The night Evan turned up at the door with groceries (see Chapter 1), we had been dating for two weeks.

> **EVAN:** I could see the struggles Karen was having. Little clues, like the first time we went out for dinner, I got the impression it was a rare treat for her.
>
> When I came to visit, I brought the groceries because I wanted to make dinner, and I wasn't just going to turn up empty-handed and eat her food. I brought food with me so I could prepare a meal and leave a little extra to fill the fridge. I brought fire logs, too, because the last time I'd visited she had put her last log on the fire. I was in the drugstore buying stuff for myself, and I saw they had logs on sale—$16 a case instead of the usual $23—so it felt natural to get a couple of cases for her.
>
> I changed her bulbs to LED because I'd noticed that Ryan had a habit of leaving all the lights on wherever he went in the house. With the old style 60W she was using, that was just burning money.

A lot of how Evan thinks is about the way his mother raised him. She would never turn up anywhere for dinner empty handed. She raised Evan and his siblings to help out around the house.

Of course, not everyone is as good at noticing things as Evan is: Evan is quite intuitive, but some people can miss things unless they're spelled out for them.

It comes down to paying attention and watching. It's about making your partner a priority and constantly thinking *how can I help this person?*

> **KAREN:** The other day, there wasn't a cold beer in the fridge for Evan when he got home from work. It's one of his little comforts in life, and I'd been home all day, but I hadn't noticed. Now that the boys are old enough to drink, they have a habit of taking beer from the fridge and not replacing it, which drives him nuts! So I will keep an eye on it moving forward, as it is one simple little thing that is important to him. I don't want to see him frustrated again when he gets home.

And, yes, sometimes your partner needs to ask.

Ryan's New Glove

One of Ryan's relatives had just given him an expensive new baseball glove for the start of the season.

Boys will be boys, and one day after practice, Ryan was goofing around with some of his teammates, and he left the glove somewhere on the baseball field.

A couple of days later, when he was getting his bag ready for a game, Ryan looked for the glove, but he couldn't find it anywhere.

"When did you last see it?" Karen asked.

"On Monday, at practice," Ryan said. "We all threw our gloves up in the air at the end."

"Did you pick it up?" his mom asked.

"I don't remember," Ryan answered, sheepishly.

It was now Wednesday.

Evan drove Ryan to the baseball field, but—surprise, surprise—it was nowhere to be found.

Ryan was worried sick.

On the drive home, Evan asked, "Do you remember what kind of glove it was?"

Luckily, Ryan remembered exactly what model it was, and the shop that it came from, so Evan drove him straight there, found an identical glove, and bought it for him.

Although it was only about nine months into the relationship, Evan wanted Ryan to know he was someone he could count on and would be there when he needed him.

Picking up on clues

Even now, ten years into the relationship, Evan still focuses on *the little things*.

Every payday, the first thing he does is go grocery shopping for the family, and he'll set himself a quest to come home with something new: a new chocolate bar, or a new gluten-free cookie or loaf. Even if it means going to a few different stores on the way home, he'll keep going until he completes his quest.

> **KAREN:** One night he came home with garlic and herb spreadable cheese. We had been to a friend's birthday party, and Evan noticed that I had spread some soft cheese on rice crackers and really liked it. The first pack he bought was wrong: cranberry and pepper. I tried hard to like it, but I just couldn't convince my taste buds!

> He didn't get offended or say something like, "Jeez, I tried to do something nice for her, and all she did was complain."
>
> Instead, he just thought *OK, course correct here. Apparently, that one is an acquired taste, but I'm determined to find the one that she likes.* I told him what the package looked like, and the next time he brought the right one home, and it was delicious.

And it's not all about food. Let's not forget the heated toilet seat (in chapter 9)! Some of the other 'little things':

- We have an aging cat that likes to sleep on Evan's side of the bed (or maybe it's Evan that likes to sleep on the cat's side of the bed!). Some husbands would shoo the cat away. Evan tolerates her and shares his side of the bed with her.

- We'll take turns to pick up coffee for each other on the way home if we've been out.

- At a Christmas party some years ago, Karen asked to see the gluten free menu. Not wanting Karen to feel *different*, Evan ordered the same as Karen was having.

The key is to be in tune with your partner's needs, whether that is a block of cheese, a waffle cone, clearing the walkway or de-icing their car. If a husband brushed the snow off his wife's car and left a note on her steering wheel to say "Hope you have a good day today. See you when you get home" it would speak volumes. Little things mean a lot.

By the same token, husbands shouldn't be afraid to tell their wife what they would like. If your wife has done something that pleased you, acknowledge it. Compliment her on what she is already doing right: "I love that casserole you made, can you make it again next week?" "I enjoyed having my mother over yesterday. I'm glad you guys got to bond."

> **EVAN:** My mother lives out east, so she and Karen hadn't really had a chance to interact. Even when we got married, there was so much to do that the two of them didn't really get to know each other.
>
> We finally got to go down and spend a whole week with her, and it meant a lot to me that Karen sat with her, listened to her dreams, and listened to her talk about my dad.

When it comes to the other way around, most men are less intuitive and attuned than Evan, so wives do need to be quite blatant in telling their husband what to do. Simply saying that something your husband did was nice could be interpreted as a thank you, and he may not realize that you're also saying "please do it again." So, tell him in a nice way what is important to you and what you want help with.

If you are feeling that it's all too much—you are working, cooking, dealing with the kids, making their lunches—then instead of getting exhausted and cranky, say "I might seem a little overwhelmed to you, because I need help. This is too much; can you help with this?"

Many women take the view, "You should notice. I shouldn't have to tell you: you should know." The reality is, you have to ask for help. Otherwise, most men don't realize.

> **KAREN:** The chances are that your husband hasn't realized what was happening and if you ask him to help, he'll say "Oh, OK!"

For example, if you are having company over and you are feeling overwhelmed, ask for help. Perhaps your husband could vacuum, or set the table, or pick up some items from the shops that were missed.

He can get his own beer!

Some people might be thinking at this point that we are suggesting you become subservient to your partner.

That's not the case at all. This is about both of you doing things for each other.

Rating

On a scale of 1-10, how good are you at supporting your partner?

On a scale of 1-10, how good is your partner at knowing your wants and needs?

Question

What are three things you could do in the next week to make your partner's week easier?

Making this work

- Each of you makes a list of five things your partner does that you appreciate and five things they do that you don't like. Swap lists and act on them, and see how it works. Simple things like, "You made breakfast last weekend, and I liked it. Can we do that again?" "Stop leaving your dirty socks in the dining room!" You'd be surprised how small it can be, but how big an impact it can have on your relationship.

- Have a conversation about expectations and boundaries. Discuss what it means to you to put 'quality' into the relationship.

- Stick to your word. If you say something is OK, don't throw it back in your partner's face later.

- Tell your partner you are blocking off one hour of your time for them and ask what they would like help with.

- If you see your partner doing a task regularly, ask them if they would like you to take over doing it for a while. It could be a simple as making the bed, loading or unloading the dishwasher, or cleaning the kitchen table.

Chapter 16

QIQO

A high-quality relationship is one where your partner respects you and values your opinion. When that happens, you have a high-quality relationship. It's a relationship that you want to keep, with someone you want to have in your life and you want to spend time with.

That kind of relationship, however, requires give as well as take. Whatever you want to get out of a relationship, you have to put into it as well: it's what we call "QIQO": "quality in, quality out."

So, if you want to be respected by your partner, you have to respect them. If you want your opinion valued, you have to value your partner's opinion.

It's an exchange of energy: put positive energy in, and you get positive energy back. Put negative energy in, and you'll get negative energy back.

It's like a bank account: you have to keep making deposits as well as withdrawals. If you make too many withdrawals without putting something back in, eventually you'll end up overdrawn, and there's a price to pay.

If you find yourself in a relationship where you are constantly putting in positive energy and only get back negative energy, then the relationship is obviously out of balance.

And if your partner is putting in positive energy and all they get back from you is negative energy, then beware: at some point, they will get fed up, and might go looking for that positive energy somewhere else!

But let's get back to healthy relationships.

The sense of reciprocity, of wanting to put in positive energy because you're going to get positive energy back begins with the conviction that you are a team, that you are in 'this' (whatever your 'this' may be) together.

One of you has to get the ball rolling, of course, but when you do, things pick up very quickly. The problem is that most people like to play it cool at the start of a new relationship. First, they don't want to appear too eager. Second, if they've been hurt before then, quite understandably, they want to see how things pan out before throwing themselves into the relationship wholeheartedly.

There's nothing wrong with that. Just be aware that if you both keep that up for too long, the relationship will never get out of the friend zone.

So much for new relationships. What about relationships that have been going for a while? It's surprisingly easy for marriages and long-term relationships to slip back into the friend zone. You get used to being around each other, so when you see each other, the spark gets a little dimmer each time. You wake up next to each other for the 3,000th time, and it doesn't feel any different from #2,999—or #2,000 for that matter. And it happens because, over time, one of you puts in high-quality positive energy and instead of getting the same or more back, you get just a little less. Not because your partner isn't committed, but just because it's easy to sit back and let things slide when you've been together for a long time. But then you realize you can let things slide, too, so you put in a little less, and you get less back in return. Before you know it, you're both sliding in a slow spiral downwards.

That's why we both put so much energy into keeping things fresh and making sure that we keep the momentum going upwards in our relationship.

The good news is, it's much easier to recapture the energy that got you together in the first place than it is to create that energy from nothing.

So, if you are playing for keeps and you know that you are with the person you want to spend the rest of your life with, but you've let things slide a little, decide that *now is where the slide stops*. Decide right now that this is where you are going to put high quality in once more, knowing that, if your partner is equally committed, you'll get high quality back from them.

You also get the satisfaction of knowing that you are treating your partner as you would like to be treated; that you are doing the best you possibly could do; and if that person, for whatever reason, isn't giving back to you, that's about them. It's their issue, not yours, because you've done your best.

This reciprocity is the foundation that our relationship is built on.

You also need to remember to do it for yourself. A lot of women drain themselves because they are trying to do too much with the children, the house, the job, etc. You have to remember to give yourself quality and positive energy, as well as everyone around you.

So how do you do that without being accused of being a lackluster employee, mother, wife, daughter, sister or whatever?

It comes down to valuing yourself and respecting yourself; knowing that if you take some time out to recharge your batteries, you are actually going to be giving more back, so it will be more beneficial to your family/work/people around you and yourself. Running yourself into the ground isn't helping anybody: it is depleting. You have to take a step back and take the time to appreciate yourself.

Don't be afraid to ask your partner for help. Give them a choice of what that help could look like, but ask for help.

For husbands, it starts with recognizing the emotional investment your wife is making in the relationship. That can be a challenge for many husbands, because—let's face it—they typically don't like to talk about emotions.

An easy way to get things going is *date night*. Even if you have a hectic life, you need to set aside time together and say, "This is going to be our date night." Even if it is just one date a month, set that time aside and hold each other accountable for keeping that date.

It's important that you plan that date, just like you would have done if you were still dating: go to a movie or a concert, go to dinner, see a show. Alternate who chooses the activity for date night, and if your partner chooses something you don't find exciting, bear in mind they may not have been over the moon with all your choices either.

Here are some ideas you could try for date night:

- Dinner at a nice restaurant
- 'Picnic' at home
- Explore a new food you haven't tried. Like sushi or tapas
- Go to a ball game
- Watch a play
- Go to a concert

You can also organize a whole date *day* occasionally, rather than just date night. Make a trip of it, or go to a spa together—many spas offer couples packages. Choose something that is fun and keeps the romance going: once you have something fun, you want to expand upon it.

Also, make sure you arrange the babysitter well in advance (after all, this is a regular thing, so you know it's coming up)—it would be disappointing to have to cancel date night at the last minute because you can't get a sitter!

Once a month is not very much, and some people do it once a week, or bi-weekly, but once a month is easy to maintain, and that's important.

When you do this, you have something in the relationship that you're both looking forward to. That alone changes the quality of the relationship.

Cranky Cards

Sometimes, we all have days when we can get cranky—have you ever noticed that, if you're a woman, it usually gets referred to as *b*tchy*? Whatever you call it, it happens. And it's almost always a cry for help: the person is feeling overwhelmed; they are spilling over with emotion, and that emotion is spilling over onto you. Your partner isn't lashing out at you, and they're not doing it on purpose. But it can feel like they are, and it can hurt.

When that happens, we leave each other a little card apologizing for our mood and behavior. We call them *cranky cards*, and they are a get out of jail free card if ever the recipient is cranky themselves.

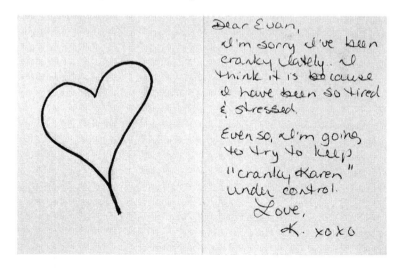

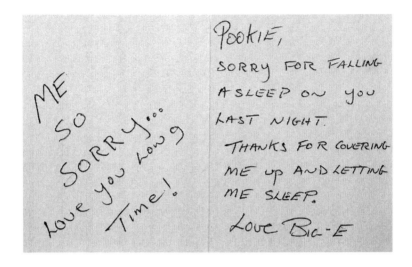

It's a fun way of defusing what could be a tense situation.

Of course, if you're getting to the point where one of you is holding so many cranky cards you could start a game of poker then you may need to look at what's going on, but otherwise, have fun with it!

"I don't feel respected"

When a man hears his wife say, "I don't feel I'm being respected," their default response is often to shut down and back away.

Remember that men are problem solvers, so rather than bringing them accusations or recriminations, bring them a problem to solve: "I need your help to figure out a problem." That approach is much more likely to make your partner feel needed or wanted; they want to be "the guy that fixes things."

Then ease into the problem by saying something like "I've been doing this… and this… and this… around the house and I'm exhausted. Is there any possible way I could get you to take one of these tasks or could you pick up the kids from school tomorrow?"

You can also add a little reverse psychology. Remember that men like to have choices, and they can be very competitive: "Which of these tasks could you excel at? Which could you do better than me?

The Boomerang Effect

Even if a relationship is struggling, that doesn't mean that both partners can't agree that it is worth working at and then both put effort—and 'quality'—in.

The effort you put into your marriage comes back to you. If you make both daily efforts, then you know that what you do is being reciprocated.

A marriage where one partner puts in all the effort and the other takes it is unbalanced and one-sided. Often that can happen when the marriage is already struggling, and one partner is more invested in making it work than the other. All it does is drive a wedge even further between them.

It becomes *high maintenance.* Not in the sense of "a high maintenance wife" who demands the very best of everything, but rather in the same way that a car that is not looked after regularly eventually starts to break down and need lots of maintenance.

When you are both on the same page, both putting quality in and getting quality out, both tackling and solving problems together, you have a "low maintenance" marriage.

Some people might think that our relationship is high maintenance because of all the things that we are constantly doing for each other. But they're missing the point: they are small things, and we are both doing them. We are a team.

If The Fish Don't Bite, Change Your Bait

In this book, we suggest a lot of things that you can try. The reason we make so many suggestions is simple. Some of them will work for you and some won't. And sometimes you'll find that what works for you is something we didn't suggest, but you got the idea because of something we said.

In many ways, this is like fishing. You try different bait and lures, and if the fish don't bite, you try something else.

In your marriage, keep trying things and seeing what reaction you get. The important thing is to put positive energy in with the aim of getting a positive reaction out.

Sometimes we'll meet a couple where the husband seems to be going out of his way to get a negative reaction from his wife. Often it's because they are desperate for any kind of interaction and reaction, and a negative one seems better than nothing. They're thinking, "At least we talked today."

Putting positive energy in

Positive energy isn't just about date night. It's simple things that you do to keep the relationship fresh.

It's looking after yourself; taking care of your appearance and always looking for ways to look better and feel better; looking for ways to keep the attraction going.

> **EVAN:** I am in love with Karen's inner self as well: I've come to know her on the inside as well as the outside. I know when something is bothering her; I can tune in on that; I can take

something off her plate or ask her if something is wrong, and she is willing to tell me.

We do silly, sweet things throughout the day, and focus our attention on each other. In many ways, it is like we are still dating.

EVAN: When we're alone we'll tease each other, in a fun—not a malicious—way. But if I'm teasing her too much, sometimes Karen tells me to "talk to the boobs."

Once Karen said it to me in front of her dad and his partner by mistake, and by the end of the evening Nancy was saying, "Talk to the boobs, Garth, talk to the boobs!"

Know what makes your partner happy

KAREN: My mother lost her twelve-year battle with cancer the day before Evan's 50th birthday. Needless to say, any plans we previously had to celebrate his birthday had to be put on hold. We now had a funeral and mourning to get through.

I had wanted to organize a birthday party for Evan ever since he told me that he had never had one as an adult, and a year later—shortly before Evan's 51st birthday—it dawned on me that I could still throw him a 50th birthday party. And what a surprise it would be: there was no way he would expect a 50th party on his 51st birthday!

Evan's mother was coming for a visit, so the timing worked out perfectly. Since it was supposed to be a surprise, Evan's brother and wife agreed to have the party at their place. Evan thought we were just going for a barbecue, but when he walked through the door with a tray of freshly made hamburgers and everyone yelled "Surprise!" the hamburgers almost ended up on the ceiling!

After lunch, we all watched a presentation of old photos that Evan's brother had prepared so we could all walk down memory lane with "Big E." It was a great time had by all.

We've discussed many ways in this book to put quality into your relationship. Ultimately, everything we have said is a matter of paying attention, listening to your partner, and doing something with what you heard.

Evan, for example, is not high maintenance: if there is cold beer in the house and a hockey game on the TV, he is happy. For other things, he also drops hints.

KAREN: If Evan just happens to say something like "We really haven't had a date

> night snack night in a long time, I'm going to pick up some stuff," I'm not going to make plans with my girlfriends and say "Oh I forgot, I didn't hear that." It's obviously important to him, so I remember it and follow through.

Evan's weekly quests to find something gluten free that is different or unique are another way of putting quality in.

We also enjoy cooking together, so that has become part of our quality. It's a shared responsibility, but it's also fun.

It's important to be a role model, not only for your children but for the people around you. Evan, for example, learned a lot about relationships by watching his grandparents and his aunts and uncles. They were good role models. He had three aunts and four uncles, and all of them have long happy marriages.

Many people have commented on how happy we are as a couple, because we radiate it. When we talk, we speak highly of each other. When someone asks one of us what we are doing this weekend, the answer is always something we are going to do together.

What Breaks a Marriage

If everything we have said until now is the secret to a long marriage, then you can probably guess that the opposite is what it takes to destroy one.

When you take your partner for granted, it can kill a relationship. You can't sustain a healthy relationship where one person is constantly putting in effort and energy, and the other person doesn't acknowledge it, or—even worse—is actively pushing them away and being negative.

Breaking trust will also kill a relationship. To put your heart into a relationship, only to have it stomped on, is incredibly painful. It is hard to recover from, and it makes it hard to even consider marrying someone else if you get divorced.

Rating

On a scale of 1-10, what quality are you putting into your relationship?

On a scale of 1-10, what quality is your partner putting into the relationship?

Question

What are three things you could do in the next week to put more energy, positivity, and quality into your relationship?

Making this work

- Listen and pay attention.
- Keep the fun in the relationship. Don't be afraid to play.
- Schedule a regular date night. Let your partner pick out an outfit that they think you look good in, and do the same for them. Then let the sparks fly!
- Go the extra mile on date night: play romantic music, get a bottle of wine, buy a rose. Remember, what you put in comes back to you.
- Never miss a special occasion like a birthday, Valentine's Day, anniversaries: put it in your calendar and set an electronic reminder on your smartphone.
- Start a new tradition. For example, we go to the Keg Steakhouse and Bar on our anniversary; it is something to look forward to.

Chapter 17

Now We Are Cooking

There are many things that can be dismissed as "not rocket science." It turns out, however, that gluten free cooking is. In fact, it's actually harder.

> *The convention center was packed. Karen had been fighting her way around the food show all afternoon, moving from stand to stand and—wherever she found one that said it was gluten free—sampling their goods. She was determined to find a gluten free stand that sold great tasting food.*
>
> *At one of the stands, she found a tray of little brownies. She popped one into her mouth, and it was... divine.*
>
> *"Oh my God, that's good," she said to the stallholder. "What's in it?"*
>
> *The exhibitor gave her a smile and a wink. "The secret ingredient is chickpea flour."*

As they talked, Karen found out more about her new BFF (best foodie friend).

She'd started cooking gluten free food after her two sons were diagnosed as high-functioning autistics. She had done some research and found that autistic children did better on gluten free diets, so the family had switched.

She was an ex-NASA engineer—a real rocket scientist! Even so, she'd found gluten free baking a challenge.

Karen knew exactly what she meant. It was how she'd felt for most of her life: gluten-free cooking can be very challenging and frustrating.

Marriage can feel a little like learning to cook gluten free. It's all too hard. You try stuff, and it just doesn't work. There's some missing ingredient you haven't found yet.

One of those secret ingredients, at least for us, is food. You'll have noticed that a lot of the stories in this book revolve around food: buying it, preparing it, eating it.

We often joke between ourselves that Evan loves to cook, and Karen loves to eat what he cooks!

Evan learned how to cook from his mother.

> **EVAN:** My grandmother was a wonderful cook, and to this day I still think her bread and tarts were the best in the world. My mother was the same. When we were small, my brother and sisters and I would take turns helping out in the kitchen: we'd peel the potatoes, and my mother would show us how to mash them and then add cream and butter.
>
> She wanted to make sure that we would have the life skills we needed when we grew up: how to do laundry, wash dishes, and of course, how to cook. All of us, including my brother, are pretty good cooks, and we all enjoy cooking: we don't see it as a chore.
>
> **KAREN:** Thank you, Shirley!

One thing that makes cooking enjoyable for Evan is that he sees it as just another way of providing for his family. He also loves getting compliments when he makes something new and it turns out well (like the seafood chowder you read about earlier).

Cooking can also be a great creative outlet. Some people like to paint, some like to build stuff, and others write or play music. Evan likes to get creative in the kitchen.

Seeing Evan so enthusiastic about food has also rubbed off on our sons: they'll see what Evan has made and ask him to teach them.

Starting with just what's in the cupboard, and no recipe, and turning "nothing" into "something" can actually be fun. And if both of you get involved—and possibly even the kids—it becomes a great bonding experience.

Passing those life skills on to your children is essential. As we said before, the days of the traditional household—one where the wife stayed home and cooked and cleaned and looked after the kids—are vanishing, if they haven't vanished already. Nowadays, most families need two incomes coming in to stay afloat. So, when you come home, you have to share the chores, and it will only get harder for the next generation. We owe it to them to make sure they know how to cook and clean and wash and everything else.

It's not just about them being able to eat. It's about them being able to find and keep a life mate!

Why this matters

If you want to see the sparks fly in your relationship, make a meal for your partner. When they come home to find that you have created something from nothing, and you have it ready for them, it will come back to you ten-fold. There is so much to appreciate: the effort to think of something, to go and get the ingredients, to prepare it all and then to cook it, and all because you want to make that person feel special.

If you don't feel like you're at the stage yet where you could walk into the kitchen and take over, then you can also make them feel special and appreciated just by asking them "Can you show me how to do some things around the kitchen?" Bear in mind that some women consider the kitchen their domain, and they don't want their man messing around in there without being shown some things first.

Rating

On a scale of 1-10, how comfortable are you in the kitchen?

Question

How do you express your creative side?

How can you involve your partner in that?

Making this work

- Make something for your wife, and put the effort in. Pick a night that you are going to make dinner. It can be anything, even soup and a sandwich! Do your best with the skills you have then build on it.
- Bring her a glass of wine and tell her you'll take care of the dinner dishes and putting the kids to bed.

Conclusion

Wrapping Up

We started this book by sharing the advice we received on our wedding day from people who cared about us, and now we have shared our own advice with you, because even though we have never met you, we care about you too. So, what have we shared?

1. Make the effort to keep the relationship fresh.
2. Show your partner that you care.
3. Listen (and prove it).
4. Let the world know how much you love your partner.
5. Make each other laugh.
6. Commit to making your partner feel special, and make them your #1 priority.
7. The small things count: simple things score big points.
8. Stress is toxic: help your partner by finding ways to take the stress off them.
9. Engage in conversation, and find as many ways as you can to communicate.
10. Give your partner respect, trust, and loyalty.

11. Share your passions with each other. Join in with what your partner is already doing, or find new activities to enjoy together.
12. Remember: "Happy wife (and husband!): happy life."

Ultimately, you get out what you put in: put quality in, and you'll get quality out. When we met, neither of us would have imagined that we would get married, let alone that we would be together 10 years later and that our life would have been transformed the way that it has been.

As we said earlier in the book, we have been given a gift: the gift of a second chance at happiness.

We hope that the lessons we learned can help you to achieve that first time round, and that you can enjoy what we have: a happy life.

JOIN THE FUN

Come and join the fun on our Facebook page–you'll find a quiz like the ones we used to get to know each other better, as well as more stories and ideas to help you keep each other happy.

www.facebook.com/howmyhusbandkeepsmehappy/

Made in the USA
Middletown, DE
25 March 2017